Tyrants of Africa: A Comprehensive History of Notorious Dictators

Copyright Page

TITLE: Tyrants of Africa: A Comprehensive History of Notorious Dictators

1ST Edition

Copyright @ 2023

Roberto M. Rodriguez. All rights reserved.

ISBN: 9798223058274

Table of Contents

Tyrants of Africa: A Comprehensive History of Notorious Dictators

By Roberto Miguel Rodriguez

Chapter 1: History of the Rise and Fall of Notorious African Dictators

Introduction to African Dictatorships

African history is marked by a series of notorious dictators who rose to power through various means and ruled their countries with an iron fist. In this subchapter, we will delve into the intriguing and often tragic stories of some of the most infamous African dictators, exploring their rise to power, the methods they employed to maintain control, and ultimately, their downfall. Through examining the histories of these dictators, we aim to shed light on the complex dynamics that have shaped the continent and its people.

The rise and fall of Idi Amin in Uganda serves as an emblematic example of the extreme brutality and anarchic rule that characterized many African dictatorships. Amin's regime was marked by widespread human rights abuses, economic mismanagement, and regional conflicts. Similarly, Mobutu Sese Seko's reign in the Democratic Republic of Congo was characterized by corruption, nepotism, and the looting of national resources. We will explore the factors that allowed these dictators to gain and maintain power, as well as the consequences of their rule for their respective countries.

Robert Mugabe's long and controversial tenure as the leader of Zimbabwe offers a unique perspective on the complexities of African politics. Initially hailed as a hero of the liberation struggle, Mugabe's regime gradually deteriorated into one of repression, economic collapse, and widespread human rights abuses. We will delve into the circumstances that led to Mugabe's rise to power, his policies, and the factors that ultimately led to his downfall.

The eccentric and enigmatic Muammar Gaddafi, who ruled Libya for over four decades, left an indelible mark on the country and the region. Gaddafi's rule was characterized by a mix of pan-Africanist ideology, authoritarianism, and repression. We will analyze the complex dynamics that allowed Gaddafi to maintain his grip on power for so long, as well as the events that led to his eventual demise.

The histories of Mengistu Haile Mariam in Ethiopia, Charles Taylor in Liberia, Jean-Bédel Bokassa in the Central African Republic, Yahya Jammeh in Gambia, Omar al-Bashir in Sudan, and Hissène Habré in Chad also offer valuable insights into the dynamics of African dictatorships. Each leader had their own unique methods of consolidating power and suppressing dissent, leaving lasting legacies of political instability and economic ruin.

By examining the rise and fall of these notorious African dictators, we hope to provide historians, diplomats, and politicians with a comprehensive understanding of the complex factors that have shaped the continent. Through understanding the histories of these dictators, we can gain valuable insights into the challenges facing African nations as they strive for democracy, human rights, and sustainable development.

Factors Leading to the Rise of Dictatorship in Africa

Title: Factors Leading to the Rise of Dictatorship in Africa

Introduction:

The African continent has witnessed the rise and fall of numerous notorious dictators throughout its history. Understanding the factors that contributed to their ascent is crucial in comprehending the complex dynamics of power and politics in Africa. This subchapter explores the common elements that led to the rise of dictatorship in Africa, drawing from the histories of infamous African dictators such as Idi Amin, Mobutu Sese Seko, Robert Mugabe, Muammar Gaddafi, Mengistu Haile Mariam, Charles Taylor, Jean-Bédel Bokassa, Yahya Jammeh, Omar al-Bashir, and Hissène Habré.

Historical Context:

To grasp the rise of dictatorship in Africa, one must consider the historical context within which these dictators emerged. Many African countries experienced colonization, followed by a struggle for independence. The transition from colonial rule to self-governance was often marred by political instability, economic challenges, and social divisions. These factors created fertile ground for individuals with authoritarian tendencies to exploit power vacuums and manipulate the nascent political systems.

Political Instability and Weak Institutions:

One of the key factors contributing to the rise of dictatorship in Africa is the prevalence of political instability and the weakness of institutions. Many African nations faced internal conflicts, coups, and civil wars, resulting in a fragmented political landscape. Weak institutions, including judiciary systems and independent media, allowed dictators to consolidate power, suppress opposition, and control the narrative.

Economic Factors:

Economic mismanagement and corruption played a significant role in fostering dictatorships in Africa. The exploitation of natural resources, such as oil, diamonds, and minerals, often led to vast wealth accumulation by ruling elites while the majority of the population remained impoverished. Economic disparities, coupled with widespread poverty and unemployment, created a breeding ground for populist leaders promising stability and prosperity, ultimately leading to the rise of dictators.

Ethnic and Tribal Divisions:

Ethnic and tribal divisions have also been exploited by dictators to consolidate power. By manipulating these divisions, dictators can maintain control over their respective ethnic groups, fostering a sense of loyalty and fear. This strategy often leads to the marginalization and oppression of minority groups, exacerbating social tensions and perpetuating cycles of violence.

Conclusion:

The rise of dictatorship in Africa can be attributed to a combination of historical, political, economic, and social factors. Understanding these factors is vital for historians, diplomats, and politicians to comprehend the complexities of power dynamics and work towards fostering democracy, good governance, and respect for human rights in Africa. By learning from the past, we can strive to prevent the rise of future dictators and promote a more prosperous and inclusive future for the continent.

The Impact of Colonialism on African Dictatorships

Colonialism has had a profound and lasting impact on African nations, shaping their political landscapes and contributing to the rise of notorious dictators. This subchapter seeks to explore the complex relationship between colonialism and the emergence of African dictatorships, focusing on key figures such as Idi Amin, Mobutu Sese Seko, Robert Mugabe, Muammar Gaddafi, Mengistu Haile Mariam, Charles Taylor, Jean-Bédel Bokassa, Yahya Jammeh, Omar al-Bashir, and Hissène Habré.

One cannot fully comprehend the rise of these dictators without first examining the legacy of colonial rule. European powers, in their scramble for Africa, imposed artificial borders, exploited resources, and established institutions that perpetuated inequality and division. This legacy created fertile ground for the emergence of authoritarian leaders who exploited these pre-existing conditions to consolidate power.

Idi Amin's brutal regime in Uganda, for example, can be traced back to the British colonial administration's policy of favoring certain ethnic groups over others. Similarly, Mobutu Sese Seko rose to power in the Democratic Republic of Congo by exploiting the power vacuum left by Belgian colonial rule. These dictators tapped into existing grievances and manipulated ethnic tensions, often exacerbating them for their own gain.

Furthermore, the colonial legacy also left African nations with weak institutions and a lack of democratic traditions. This provided dictators with the opportunity to consolidate power and suppress dissent. Robert Mugabe's long rule in Zimbabwe is a prime example of this, as he exploited the country's post-colonial transition to amass power and silence opposition.

Additionally, the influence of external powers cannot be ignored when examining the impact of colonialism on African dictatorships. Leaders such as Muammar Gaddafi and Mengistu Haile Mariam were propped up by foreign support, enabling them to maintain their grip on power despite widespread human rights abuses.

Understanding the impact of colonialism on African dictatorships is crucial for historians, diplomats, and politicians alike. By recognizing the deep-rooted causes of these dictatorships, efforts can be made to address the underlying issues of inequality, ethnic tensions, and weak institutions. Only through this understanding can the cycle of authoritarian rule be broken and a path towards democracy and stability be forged.

In conclusion, the legacy of colonialism looms large over the history of African dictatorships. The artificial borders, exploitation of resources, and the legacy of inequality left by colonial powers created fertile ground for the rise of authoritarian leaders. By analyzing the specific cases of Idi Amin, Mobutu Sese Seko, Robert Mugabe, Muammar Gaddafi, Mengistu Haile Mariam, Charles Taylor, Jean-Bédel Bokassa, Yahya Jammeh, Omar al-Bashir, and Hissène Habré, this subchapter sheds light on the complex relationship between colonialism and African dictatorships. It is essential for historians, diplomats, and politicians to understand these dynamics in order to address the root causes of authoritarian rule and work towards a more democratic and stable Africa.

The Role of Cold War Politics in African Dictatorships

Introduction:

The African continent witnessed the rise and fall of numerous notorious dictators during the 20th century. These autocrats, such as Idi Amin, Mobutu Sese Seko, Robert Mugabe, Muammar Gaddafi, Mengistu Haile Mariam, Charles Taylor, Jean-Bédel Bokassa, Yahya Jammeh, Omar al-Bashir, and Hissène Habré, left an indelible mark on their respective nations. However, to truly comprehend the complexities of their reigns, it is essential to delve into the role of Cold War politics in shaping African dictatorships.

Cold War Politics and Its Influence:

The Cold War era, characterized by ideological rivalries between the United States and the Soviet Union, had profound implications for African nations. These rival superpowers sought to expand their spheres of influence, leading to a series of proxy conflicts on the African continent. In this turbulent environment, many dictators emerged, exploiting the power vacuum and political instability to consolidate their rule.

During the Cold War, the United States and the Soviet Union provided military and economic aid to African countries, often favoring leaders who aligned with their respective ideologies. This support bolstered the regimes of dictators, enabling them to suppress dissent and maintain control over their nations.

Impact on African Dictatorships:

The Cold War politics heavily influenced the rise and fall of African dictators. For instance, Mobutu Sese Seko of the Democratic Republic of Congo received substantial support from the United States due to his staunch anti-communist stance. This assistance allowed him to rule with an iron fist for over three decades, causing immense suffering for the Congolese people.

Similarly, Idi Amin of Uganda exploited Cold War rivalries by aligning himself with Arab nations and the Soviet Union. He used this support to perpetrate human rights abuses and pursue aggressive foreign policies, leading to the collapse of the Ugandan economy and widespread violence.

Even after the Cold War, the remnants of this political rivalry continued to shape African dictatorships. Robert Mugabe of Zimbabwe, for instance, maintained his grip on power for decades through a combination of repression and populist policies. His anti-colonial rhetoric appealed to African nations that were still grappling with the legacy of colonialism.

Conclusion:

In conclusion, the role of Cold War politics in African dictatorships cannot be underestimated. The support provided by rival superpowers created an enabling environment for autocrats to rise and maintain their power. The consequences of their rule, marked by human rights abuses, economic mismanagement, and political instability, continue to haunt the African continent. By understanding the intricate dynamics of Cold War politics, historians, diplomats, and politicians can gain valuable insights into the history of these notorious African dictators and the broader context in which they operated.

The Influence of Ethnic and Tribal Politics on African Dictatorships

Ethnic and tribal politics have played a significant role in shaping the rise and fall of notorious African dictators throughout history. This subchapter delves into the intricate relationship between ethnic and tribal dynamics and the dictatorial regimes that have plagued the African continent.

In many African countries, ethnic and tribal divisions are deeply ingrained, with various ethnic groups vying for power and resources. Dictators often exploit these divisions to consolidate their control and maintain their grip on power. By leveraging ethnic loyalties, they manipulate and manipulate rivalries to their advantage, perpetuating a cycle of violence and oppression.

One notable example is Idi Amin, the former dictator of Uganda. Amin capitalized on the historical tensions between the ethnic groups of Uganda, particularly the Baganda and the Acholi, to justify his brutal regime. He strategically appointed members of his own ethnic group, the Kakwa, to key positions of power, further deepening ethnic divisions and sowing seeds of discord among the population.

Similarly, Mobutu Sese Seko of the Democratic Republic of Congo exploited ethnic rivalries to maintain his dictatorship. Mobutu favored his own ethnic group, the Ngbandi, and marginalized other ethnic communities, leading to widespread resentment and unrest. The resulting ethnic conflicts not only served to divert attention from Mobutu's oppressive regime but also weakened any potential opposition.

Robert Mugabe, the former leader of Zimbabwe, also employed tribal politics to consolidate his power. Mugabe, a member of the Shona ethnic group, used his position to discriminate against the Ndebele ethnic group, leading to mass killings and human rights abuses. By fueling ethnic tensions, Mugabe sought to maintain control and suppress any opposition.

The influence of ethnic and tribal politics is not limited to these examples alone. Throughout the history of African dictatorships, leaders like Muammar Gaddafi in Libya, Mengistu Haile Mariam in Ethiopia, Charles Taylor in Liberia, Jean-Bédel Bokassa in the Central African Republic, Yahya Jammeh in Gambia, Omar al-Bashir in Sudan, and Hissène Habré in Chad exploited ethnic divisions to perpetuate their oppressive rule.

Understanding the role of ethnic and tribal politics in African dictatorships is crucial for historians, diplomats, and politicians. By recognizing the complexities of these dynamics, we can gain a deeper understanding of the causes and consequences of dictatorship in Africa. Furthermore, this knowledge can inform future efforts to promote peace, stability, and democracy in the continent, ultimately breaking the cycle of dictatorial rule.

Chapter 2: History of the Rise and Fall of Idi Amin (Uganda)

Early Life and Background of Idi Amin

Idi Amin, one of the most infamous dictators in African history, was born in 1925 in the small village of Koboko, located in northwestern Uganda. His father was a member of the Kakwa ethnic group, and his mother belonged to the Lugbara tribe. Growing up in a polygamous household, Amin experienced a turbulent childhood, marked by poverty and family struggles.

Little is known about his early education, but it is believed that Amin attended a missionary school where he learned to read, write, and speak English fluently. This basic education would later prove instrumental in his rise to power and interactions with the international community.

In 1946, Amin joined the King's African Rifles (KAR), a regiment of the British colonial army. His military career quickly flourished, and he served in various positions, including as a cook and a heavyweight boxing champion. Amin's physical prowess and charisma earned him the respect and admiration of his fellow soldiers.

During his time in the KAR, Amin participated in several military campaigns, including the Mau Mau Uprising in Kenya and the Congo Crisis. These experiences further solidified his military skills and allowed him to establish connections with influential individuals within the army.

In 1971, while President Obote was attending a Commonwealth summit in Singapore, Amin seized the opportunity to stage a military coup. With the support of the army, Amin toppled Obote's government and declared himself the President of Uganda. This marked the beginning of a brutal and tyrannical regime that would last for eight years.

Amin's rule was characterized by widespread human rights abuses, political repression, and economic mismanagement. He targeted ethnic and political minorities, leading to the deaths of an estimated 300,000 people. Amin's erratic behavior and grandiose ambitions also strained Uganda's relationships with other countries, earning him the reputation of a ruthless and unpredictable dictator.

In 1979, Amin's regime was overthrown by a coalition of Ugandan exiles and Tanzanian forces. He fled to Saudi Arabia, where he lived in exile until his death in 2003.

The early life and background of Idi Amin provide crucial insights into the factors that shaped his personality and set the stage for his brutal dictatorship. Understanding Amin's upbringing and military career is essential for historians, diplomats, and politicians seeking to comprehend the rise and fall of one of Africa's most notorious dictators.

Amin's Ascendancy to Power

In the annals of African history, the rise to power of notorious dictators has left an indelible mark on the continent. One such figure, who etched his name into the darkest chapters of Uganda's past, was Idi Amin. This subchapter delves into Amin's ascendancy to power, dissecting the events that led to his dictatorial rule and the subsequent consequences that befell the nation.

Idi Amin's rise to power can be traced back to January 25, 1971, when he orchestrated a military coup that ousted President Obote from office. Amin, a former army officer, capitalized on the discontent within the military ranks and exploited ethnic divisions to rally support for his cause. This marked the beginning of a reign that would be characterized by brutality, human rights abuses, and economic mismanagement.

Amin's seizure of power was met with mixed reactions, both domestically and internationally. While some celebrated his coup as a necessary change, others were quick to recognize the danger his rule posed. Historians and political analysts have since grappled with understanding the factors that enabled Amin to consolidate his power so swiftly and maintain his grip on Uganda for the next eight years.

One key element of Amin's rise was his ability to manipulate tribal tensions to his advantage. By exploiting deep-seated ethnic rivalries, Amin was able to solidify his support base within the military and among certain tribes, while marginalizing others. This strategy not only ensured his survival but also contributed to the destabilization of Uganda's social fabric, leading to years of violence and division.

Amin's ascent to power was also facilitated by his cunning manipulation of international relationships. Despite his erratic behavior and flagrant human rights abuses, Amin managed to maintain a semblance of support from certain foreign powers, who saw him as a strategic ally in the region. This support, coupled with Amin's ability to control and suppress dissent, allowed him to consolidate his dictatorial rule and evade international intervention.

The consequences of Amin's ascendancy to power were catastrophic for Uganda. His regime was marked by gross human rights violations, including the massacre of an estimated 300,000 people. Additionally, Amin's economic mismanagement plunged the country into turmoil, leading to hyperinflation, food shortages, and a collapsing infrastructure.

The rise to power of dictators like Idi Amin serves as a cautionary tale for historians, diplomats, and politicians. It highlights the importance of understanding the complex dynamics that enable such figures to come to power and the devastating consequences that follow. By studying these historical cases, we can gain valuable insights into the factors that contribute to the rise and fall of notorious African dictators, ultimately informing our efforts to prevent such atrocities in the future.

Amin's Reign of Terror and Human Rights Violations

One of the most notorious dictators in African history, Idi Amin's reign of terror in Uganda left a lasting impact on the nation and its people. Amin's rise to power was marked by violence and brutality, and his regime was characterized by widespread human rights violations.

During his eight-year rule from 1971 to 1979, Amin's regime was responsible for the deaths of an estimated 300,000 Ugandans. Political opponents, intellectuals, and anyone perceived as a threat to his power were targeted and executed. Amin's security forces, known as the State Research Bureau, carried out these acts of violence with impunity.

Human rights violations were rampant under Amin's rule, with reports of torture, forced disappearances, and mass killings becoming commonplace. The infamous "killing fields" of Uganda witnessed countless atrocities, as Amin's henchmen carried out systematic campaigns of violence against ethnic minorities, particularly the Acholi and Lango tribes.

Amin's brutal tactics extended beyond Uganda's borders. He invaded Tanzania in 1978, leading to the Uganda-Tanzania War, which resulted in the overthrow of his regime. During this conflict, Amin's forces committed numerous war crimes, including the indiscriminate bombing of civilian areas and the use of child soldiers.

The international community, including historians, diplomats, and politicians, widely condemned Amin's reign of terror and human rights abuses. The United Nations and various human rights organizations documented the atrocities committed under his rule, shining a light on the horrors endured by the Ugandan people.

Amin's reign of terror serves as a stark reminder of the dangers of unchecked power and the devastating consequences for human rights. His brutal regime left behind a legacy of fear, trauma, and division in Uganda, one that the nation continues to grapple with today.

The story of Amin's reign of terror is not unique in the history of African dictators. Throughout the continent, notorious leaders like Mobutu Sese Seko, Robert Mugabe, Muammar Gaddafi, Mengistu Haile Mariam, Charles Taylor, Jean-Bédel Bokassa, Yahya Jammeh, Omar al-Bashir, and Hissène Habré have also left a trail of human rights violations and suffering in their wake.

By studying the rise and fall of these notorious African dictators, historians, diplomats, and politicians can gain a deeper understanding of the complex dynamics that contribute to the rise of authoritarian regimes. It is through this understanding that we can work towards preventing such atrocities in the future and ensuring the protection of human rights for all.

Amin's Foreign Policy and Relations with the International Community

One cannot discuss the history of notorious African dictators without delving into the complex foreign policies and relations they maintained with the international community. In this subchapter, we will explore Amin's foreign policy during his reign as the dictator of Uganda and his interactions with the global stage.

Idi Amin's rule in Uganda, from 1971 to 1979, was marked by a distinct brand of erratic and often unpredictable foreign policy. Amin's rise to power was met with both curiosity and concern from the international community. As historians, diplomats, and politicians, it is essential to understand the dynamics of his foreign relations.

Amin's early years in power were characterized by a desire to assert Uganda's independence and challenge the influence of former colonial powers. He expelled the Asian population, mainly of Indian descent, from Uganda, seizing their businesses and properties. This move was met with outrage and condemnation from the international community, leading to strained relations with various countries, particularly Britain and India.

Despite these tensions, Amin sought alliances with other African nations, particularly those in the Organization of African Unity (OAU). He positioned himself as a champion of African unity and anti-imperialism, which resonated with several African leaders. Amin's charisma and theatrical diplomacy allowed him to build alliances with countries like Libya, where he forged a close relationship with Muammar Gaddafi.

However, Amin's foreign policy was often marked by grandiose gestures and questionable decisions. He declared himself the "Conqueror of the British Empire" and sought to position Uganda as a global power. This resulted in strained relations with Western countries, who viewed Amin's regime as destabilizing and unpredictable.

Amin's international reputation became further tarnished by allegations of human rights abuses and his decision to support various rebel groups in neighboring countries. He provided support to separatist movements in Tanzania and Sudan, further exacerbating regional tensions and drawing international condemnation.

In conclusion, Amin's foreign policy and relations with the international community were characterized by a mix of grandiose gestures, erratic decision-making, and alliances with other African nations. His rule drew both curiosity and concern from the global stage, with his actions often straining relations with Western countries. Understanding Amin's foreign policy is crucial in comprehending the complex dynamics of his dictatorship and its impact on Uganda and the wider African continent.

The Downfall and Exile of Idi Amin

Idi Amin, one of the most notorious African dictators, rose to power in Uganda in 1971 through a military coup. Known for his brutal regime and eccentric behavior, Amin's rule was marked by violence, corruption, and human rights abuses. However, his reign came to a dramatic end, resulting in his eventual exile from the country.

Amin's downfall can be attributed to a combination of factors, including his aggressive foreign policies, economic mismanagement, and growing international pressure. His invasion of Tanzania in 1978, aimed at annexing the Kagera region, led to a full-scale war with Tanzania and the Ugandan exile community known as the Uganda National Liberation Army (UNLA). The conflict weakened Amin's hold on power and exposed his military incompetence.

Simultaneously, Amin's mismanagement of the economy resulted in hyperinflation, scarcity of essential goods, and widespread poverty. The Ugandan people grew increasingly discontented as their living conditions deteriorated, fueling opposition groups and dissent within the military.

Internationally, Amin's erratic behavior and human rights abuses drew condemnation from the international community. His expulsion of thousands of Ugandan Asians and the brutal massacre of the Acholi and Lango ethnic groups tarnished his reputation. The United Nations and various human rights organizations exerted pressure on Amin, imposing economic sanctions and isolating Uganda diplomatically.

In 1979, a coalition of Tanzanian and Ugandan exile forces launched a successful military campaign to overthrow Amin's regime. Supported by the Tanzanian army, the UNLA advanced towards Kampala, the capital city, while Amin's forces crumbled under the pressure. Faced with a humiliating defeat, Amin fled Uganda in April 1979, seeking refuge first in Libya and later in Saudi Arabia.

Amin's exile in Saudi Arabia lasted until his death in 2003. Despite numerous calls for his extradition to face trial for his crimes, Saudi authorities provided him with protection, citing political reasons. Amin lived the remainder of his life in relative obscurity, far from the power and influence he once enjoyed.

The downfall and exile of Idi Amin serve as a cautionary tale about the consequences of unchecked power and the importance of international pressure in holding dictators accountable. It also highlights the resilience of the Ugandan people and their determination to rid their country of a tyrant. Amin's legacy continues to haunt Uganda, but it also reminds the world of the importance of upholding human rights and promoting democratic values.

Chapter 3: History of the Rise and Fall of Mobutu Sese Seko (Democratic Republic of Congo)

Mobutu's Early Life and Political Career

In the annals of African dictators, few names evoke as much intrigue and controversy as Mobutu Sese Seko. Born Joseph-Désiré Mobutu on October 14, 1930, in Lisala, Belgian Congo, he would go on to become one of the longest-serving and most notorious rulers of the Democratic Republic of Congo, formerly known as Zaire. This subchapter delves into Mobutu's early life and political career, shedding light on the factors that shaped his iron-fisted rule and ultimately led to his downfall.

Raised in a modest family, Mobutu grew up witnessing the injustices and exploitation inflicted upon his fellow Congolese by the Belgian colonizers. This experience fueled his desire to fight for the independence of his nation. As a young man, he joined the Congolese National Movement and emerged as a charismatic leader, rallying the masses with his fiery speeches and nationalist agenda.

Following the country's independence in 1960, Mobutu quickly ascended the political ladder. He initially served as Chief of Staff of the Congolese Army but soon seized power in a bloodless coup against the elected Prime Minister, Patrice Lumumba. This marked the beginning of Mobutu's autocratic rule, which would endure for the next three decades.

Embracing an ideology known as "Mobutism," he aimed to consolidate power and enrich himself at the expense of the Congolese people. Mobutu swiftly marginalized political opponents, dismantled democratic institutions, and established a cult of personality around himself. His regime was characterized by rampant corruption, human rights abuses, and economic mismanagement.

Internationally, Mobutu skillfully played Cold War rivals against each other, receiving support from both the United States and the Soviet Union. This allowed him to maintain his grip on power while exploiting the country's vast mineral wealth for personal gain. However, as the Cold War drew to a close, international support waned, and internal discontent grew.

Mobutu's political career reached its nadir in the 1990s when a wave of pro-democracy movements swept across Africa. Facing mounting pressure, he reluctantly agreed to hold multi-party elections in 1992. Nevertheless, the elections were marred by fraud and violence, and Mobutu retained his grip on power until 1997.

In conclusion, Mobutu's early life and political career laid the groundwork for his despotic rule over the Democratic Republic of Congo. From his humble beginnings to his ascent to power and subsequent reign, he left an indelible mark on African history. Understanding this chapter of Mobutu's life is crucial for historians, diplomats, and politicians interested in comprehending the rise and fall of notorious African dictators.

Mobutu's Consolidation of Power and Creation of a One-Party State

Mobutu Sese Seko, the notorious dictator of the Democratic Republic of Congo (formerly known as Zaire), rose to power in 1965 after a military coup. His reign, which lasted for over three decades, was marked by corruption, oppression, and the consolidation of his personal power.

After taking control, Mobutu quickly dismantled the existing political system and established a one-party state known as the Popular Movement of the Revolution (MPR). This move allowed him to solidify his authority and suppress any potential opposition. The MPR became the only legal political party, and all other parties were banned.

To maintain his grip on power, Mobutu employed a combination of propaganda, intimidation, and violence. He created a personality cult around himself, portraying himself as the sole savior of the nation. His image was plastered across billboards, while state-controlled media constantly praised his leadership and accomplishments.

Mobutu also used his power to amass immense wealth. He implemented a policy known as "Zairianization," which involved seizing foreign-owned assets and handing them over to his cronies and loyalists. This system of patronage allowed him to co-opt the elite and ensure their loyalty.

Furthermore, Mobutu's regime was characterized by widespread human rights abuses. Dissent was not tolerated, and anyone suspected of opposing the regime was subject to arbitrary arrest, torture, or execution. Political opponents, journalists, and activists were silenced, leaving no room for opposition or public discourse.

Despite his oppressive rule, Mobutu managed to maintain the support of some foreign powers, most notably the United States. This support was largely driven by Mobutu's anticommunist stance during the Cold War, as he positioned himself as a key ally in the region.

However, Mobutu's reign eventually crumbled under the weight of his own mismanagement and corruption. The economy collapsed, and public dissatisfaction grew. In 1997, rebel forces led by Laurent Kabila overthrew Mobutu, effectively ending his rule.

In conclusion, Mobutu's consolidation of power and creation of a one-party state in the Democratic Republic of Congo was marked by corruption, oppression, and the suppression of dissent. His reign serves as a cautionary tale of the dangers of unchecked dictatorship and the devastating consequences it can have on a nation and its people.

Mobutu's Authoritarian Rule and Economic Mismanagement

In the annals of African dictatorship, Mobutu Sese Seko's rule in the Democratic Republic of Congo stands out as a particularly egregious example of authoritarianism and economic mismanagement. From 1965 to 1997, Mobutu held a tight grip on power, suppressing dissent, plundering the nation's resources, and leaving behind a legacy of poverty and instability.

Mobutu's rise to power came after a period of political turmoil in Congo, following its independence from Belgium in 1960. Exploiting the chaos, Mobutu, then an army officer, seized control in a military coup. He quickly consolidated his power, disbanding political parties and suppressing opposition voices, effectively establishing a one-party state.

Under Mobutu's rule, corruption became rampant and widespread. He used his position to amass enormous personal wealth, while the majority of the Congolese population lived in poverty. The country's vast natural resources, including diamonds, copper, and cobalt, were exploited for personal gain rather than benefiting the nation as a whole. The economy was mismanaged, with little investment in infrastructure or social services, leading to widespread poverty and a deteriorating standard of living.

Mobutu's authoritarian regime also stifled political dissent and opposition. The media was tightly controlled, with censorship and intimidation tactics used to silence critics. Political opponents were persecuted, imprisoned, or forced into exile. The lack of political freedoms and human rights abuses under Mobutu's rule created a climate of fear and oppression.

The consequences of Mobutu's misrule were felt long after his reign ended. The economy was in shambles, with hyperinflation and a collapsing infrastructure. Social services, including healthcare and education, were severely lacking. The country's institutions were weakened, and ethnic tensions simmered beneath the surface, eventually leading to the devastating conflicts of the late 1990s and early 2000s.

Mobutu's authoritarian rule and economic mismanagement have left a lasting impact on the Democratic Republic of Congo. It serves as a cautionary tale of the dangers of unchecked power and the devastating consequences of corruption and misrule. As historians, diplomats, and politicians, it is crucial to study and understand the rise and fall of notorious African dictators like Mobutu in order to prevent such abuses of power in the future and work towards building more just and equitable societies.

Mobutu's Relationship with the West and Africa

In the tumultuous history of African dictators, Mobutu Sese Seko, the former president of the Democratic Republic of Congo, stands out as one of the most influential and controversial figures. His relationship with the West and Africa played a crucial role in shaping the destiny of his country and the wider region.

Mobutu's rise to power in 1965 marked the beginning of a new era for Congo. Initially supported by Western powers, particularly the United States, who saw him as a bulwark against communism in Africa, Mobutu quickly consolidated his grip on power. He implemented a policy of Africanization, promoting a sense of national identity and pride while marginalizing foreign influences. This resonated well with the African population, and Mobutu became a symbol of African nationalism.

However, as time went on, Mobutu's relationship with the West began to sour. His authoritarian rule, marked by rampant corruption and human rights abuses, drew criticism from international observers. Western countries, including the United States, started to distance themselves from Mobutu, who was increasingly seen as a liability rather than an ally.

At the same time, Mobutu sought to strengthen his ties with other African nations, particularly those in the Francophone bloc. He positioned himself as a leader of the Non-Aligned Movement and played a significant role in mediating conflicts in neighboring countries, such as Angola and Rwanda. This earned him respect among his African counterparts and enabled him to maintain a degree of regional influence.

However, Mobutu's attempts to project himself as a pan-African leader were met with mixed reactions. While some African leaders admired his ability to navigate the complex web of international politics, others criticized his autocratic rule and his failure to address the socio-economic challenges facing his own country.

In the end, Mobutu's relationship with both the West and Africa proved to be his downfall. The end of the Cold War and the increasing calls for democracy in Africa made it difficult for Western countries to continue supporting a dictator. Within Africa, Mobutu's diminishing legitimacy and the growing pressure for democratic reforms led to his eventual overthrow in 1997.

Mobutu's complex relationship with the West and Africa serves as a poignant reminder of the challenges faced by African dictators. It highlights the delicate balance they must strike between maintaining international support and appeasing their own people. Mobutu's story is a cautionary tale, a reminder that the pursuit of power and personal interests can have far-reaching consequences for both the leader and the nation.

The Overthrow and Death of Mobutu Sese Seko

In the annals of African history, few dictators have left as lasting an impact as Mobutu Sese Seko. Known for his iron-fisted rule and extravagant lifestyle, Mobutu's reign over the Democratic Republic of Congo (formerly Zaire) lasted for over three decades. However, his rule eventually crumbled under the weight of corruption, economic mismanagement, and popular discontent.

The rise of Mobutu can be traced back to the political turmoil that followed Congo's independence from Belgium in 1960. As a military officer, Mobutu swiftly capitalized on the power vacuum and orchestrated a coup in 1965, ousting the country's first democratically elected leader, Patrice Lumumba. From that moment on, Mobutu consolidated his grip on power, establishing a one-party state and effectively eliminating any opposition.

During his early years in power, Mobutu adopted a populist approach, presenting himself as a champion of African nationalism and promoting a policy of "authenticity." He changed the country's name to Zaire, forced citizens to adopt African names, and even renamed himself Mobutu Sese Seko Kuku Ngbendu Wa Za Banga, which roughly translates to "the all-powerful warrior who goes from conquest to conquest, leaving fire in his wake."

However, beneath the veneer of populism, Mobutu's regime was marked by rampant corruption and economic mismanagement. He ruthlessly plundered the country's vast natural resources, amassing a personal fortune while the majority of Congolese lived in abject poverty. His lavish lifestyle, complete with palaces, private jets, and a personal zoo, served as a stark contrast to the dire conditions experienced by ordinary citizens.

By the 1990s, Mobutu's rule was teetering on the edge of collapse. Widespread unrest and armed rebellions erupted across the country, fueled by the deteriorating economy and growing dissatisfaction with his autocratic rule. In 1997, Laurent Kabila, backed by a coalition of rebel groups and foreign powers, launched a successful military campaign to overthrow Mobutu.

Mobutu fled to Morocco, where he lived in exile until his death from prostate cancer in 1997. His overthrow marked the end of an era in Congolese history, but the legacy of his rule continues to haunt the country to this day. The collapse of state institutions and the emergence of armed militias in the aftermath of his reign have contributed to ongoing instability in the Democratic Republic of Congo.

The overthrow and death of Mobutu Sese Seko serve as a cautionary tale of the rise and fall of notorious African dictators. His story, alongside those of other infamous figures such as Idi Amin, Robert Mugabe, and Muammar Gaddafi, sheds light on the complexities of power, corruption, and the enduring struggle for democracy on the African continent. It is a story that historians, diplomats, and politicians must study and understand to prevent the repetition of such dark chapters in African history.

Chapter 4: History of the Rise and Fall of Robert Mugabe (Zimbabwe)

Mugabe's Early Life and Role in Zimbabwean Independence

Robert Mugabe, one of the most notorious African dictators, played a pivotal role in the history of Zimbabwe. Born on February 21, 1924, in Kutama, Southern Rhodesia (now Zimbabwe), Mugabe grew up in a society deeply impacted by British colonial rule. His early life experiences and political ideologies shaped his rise to power and subsequent iron-fisted rule over the country for nearly four decades.

Mugabe's journey towards becoming a prominent figure in Zimbabwean politics began in the 1950s when he joined the National Democratic Party (NDP), which aimed to challenge the oppressive colonial regime. Later, he became a key member of the Zimbabwe African National Union (ZANU), a political party dedicated to the liberation of Zimbabwe from British rule.

During the 1960s, Mugabe played an instrumental role in organizing and leading guerrilla warfare against the white minority government. This period marked the beginning of his reputation as a skilled strategist and charismatic leader within the liberation movement. Mugabe's determination and unwavering commitment to fighting for Zimbabwean independence earned him widespread admiration from his fellow countrymen.

Following the Lancaster House Agreement in 1979, which ended the Rhodesian Bush War, Mugabe played a crucial role in the negotiations that led to Zimbabwe's independence in 1980. As the leader of ZANU-PF, Mugabe led his party to a landslide victory in the subsequent elections, becoming the country's first prime minister.

However, Mugabe's early years as an independent Zimbabwean leader were marked by a sense of hope and optimism that would soon fade. Gradually, he consolidated power, taking advantage of his position to silence opposition and suppress dissent. Mugabe's authoritarian rule became increasingly evident through the implementation of oppressive policies, such as the seizure of white-owned farms, which resulted in economic instability and international condemnation.

Despite his initial role as a liberator and advocate for racial equality, Mugabe's later years in power were marred by corruption, human rights abuses, and economic decline. His grip on power remained unyielding, and the once prosperous nation was left impoverished and divided.

Mugabe's early life and role in Zimbabwean independence provide a crucial understanding of the complex factors that contributed to the rise and fall of this notorious African dictator. Examining his journey from a young boy in colonial Rhodesia to a dominant and authoritarian leader sheds light on the challenges faced by post-colonial African nations and the consequences of unchecked power.

Mugabe's Initial Years in Power and Promises of Prosperity

When Robert Mugabe assumed power in Zimbabwe in 1980, there was a sense of hope and optimism among the people. After years of colonial rule under British governance, Zimbabwe gained its independence, and Mugabe became the nation's first black Prime Minister. His initial years in power were marked by promises of prosperity and a vision for a united and prosperous Zimbabwe.

Mugabe's rise to power was fueled by his charisma and ability to connect with the masses. He campaigned on a platform of land redistribution, economic empowerment, and social justice. The people believed in his vision and placed their hopes in his leadership, eager to see their country flourish under his rule.

One of Mugabe's key promises was the redistribution of land from white farmers to the black majority. This policy aimed to rectify the historical injustices of colonialism and empower the previously marginalized black population. However, the execution of this policy became a contentious issue that would later contribute to the country's downfall.

In his early years, Mugabe implemented various social programs and policies to uplift the nation. He invested in education, healthcare, and infrastructure development, with the aim of improving the living standards of all Zimbabweans. These efforts were initially successful, and the country experienced a period of relative stability and economic growth.

However, as Mugabe consolidated his power, cracks began to appear in his leadership. Political repression and human rights abuses became rampant, with opposition parties and dissidents facing persecution. Mugabe's regime became increasingly authoritarian, stifling dissent and consolidating power within his ruling party, ZANU-PF.

Despite the initial promises of prosperity, Mugabe's leadership ultimately led to the economic decline of Zimbabwe. Corruption, mismanagement, and the controversial land redistribution policies contributed to a collapse in agricultural production and foreign investment. Inflation skyrocketed, unemployment soared, and poverty levels increased dramatically.

Mugabe's decades-long rule finally came to an end in 2017, when he was forced to resign amid mounting pressure from the people and the military. His legacy is one of missed opportunities and unfulfilled promises. Mugabe's initial years in power held immense potential for Zimbabwe, but as the years went by, his regime became synonymous with corruption, repression, and economic decline.

In studying the history of notorious African dictators, Mugabe's story serves as a cautionary tale. It highlights the importance of leadership that prioritizes the well-being of the people and upholds democratic values. By examining Mugabe's rise and fall, historians, diplomats, and politicians can gain valuable insights into the complex dynamics of power and the consequences of unchecked authority.

Mugabe's Land Reform Policies and Economic Crisis

Robert Mugabe, the former President of Zimbabwe, is widely known for his controversial land reform policies and their devastating impact on the country's economy. This subchapter delves into the complexities of Mugabe's land reform policies and the subsequent economic crisis that unfolded in Zimbabwe.

Mugabe's land reform policies were implemented in the early 2000s as an attempt to address the historical injustices of colonial-era land ownership. The policies aimed to redistribute land from white farmers to black Zimbabweans, who had been marginalized during the colonial period. While the goals of the land reform were noble, the execution of these policies was marred by corruption, violence, and lack of planning.

The sudden and often violent seizure of farmland from white farmers led to a significant decline in agricultural production, which had been the backbone of Zimbabwe's economy. The once-thriving agricultural sector suffered from a lack of expertise and investment, as many of the new landowners lacked the necessary skills and resources to maintain productive farms. The resulting decline in food production led to widespread food shortages and hyperinflation, with prices soaring and the Zimbabwean dollar becoming virtually worthless.

Furthermore, Mugabe's policies led to a breakdown in investor confidence and a decline in foreign direct investment. The government's disregard for property rights and the rule of law created an environment of uncertainty and instability, deterring both domestic and foreign investors from engaging in economic activities in Zimbabwe. The economy, once considered one of Africa's most promising, was pushed into a deep recession, with unemployment rates skyrocketing and poverty levels reaching alarming heights.

Mugabe's land reform policies and the subsequent economic crisis in Zimbabwe serve as a cautionary tale for other African nations grappling with issues of land ownership and inequality. The case of Zimbabwe highlights the importance of implementing land reform policies in a transparent and equitable manner, with careful consideration for the long-term economic consequences.

In conclusion, Mugabe's land reform policies had a profound and detrimental impact on Zimbabwe's economy. The violent seizure of farmland, lack of planning, and corruption led to a decline in agricultural production, hyperinflation, and a breakdown in investor confidence. This subchapter serves as a reminder of the complexities and challenges associated with land reform and the need for careful planning and implementation to avoid similar economic crises in the future.

Mugabe's Repression and Human Rights Abuses

Robert Mugabe, the former President of Zimbabwe, was one of the most notorious African dictators in history. His reign, which lasted for almost four decades, was marred by widespread repression and egregious human rights abuses. This subchapter delves into Mugabe's tyrannical rule, shedding light on the extent of his brutality and its impact on the people of Zimbabwe.

Mugabe's rise to power in the 1980s promised a bright future for Zimbabwe. However, his initial popularity quickly faded as he consolidated his power and transformed the nation into his personal fiefdom. Mugabe's regime employed various tactics to suppress dissent and maintain control. These included censorship of the media, intimidation of political opponents, and the use of violence against those who dared to challenge his authority.

Perhaps the most infamous episode of Mugabe's repression was the Gukurahundi massacre in the 1980s. In an attempt to quell opposition in the southwestern region of Matabeleland, Mugabe ordered the deployment of the North Korean-trained Fifth Brigade. This military unit carried out a campaign of terror, targeting the Ndebele ethnic group and committing mass killings, torture, and rape. The exact death toll remains unknown, but estimates suggest that up to 20,000 people lost their lives.

Mugabe's assault on human rights continued throughout his rule. He manipulated elections, rigged the judiciary, and curtailed civil liberties, effectively silencing any opposition. The media became heavily censored, and journalists critical of the regime faced harassment, imprisonment, or even death. Mugabe's land reforms, ostensibly aimed at addressing historical inequalities, were used as a tool for political patronage, leading to economic collapse and widespread poverty.

Despite the international community's condemnation of Mugabe's actions, he remained defiant until his eventual ousting in 2017. However, the legacy of his repression and human rights abuses still lingers in Zimbabwe. The country faces a long road towards healing and rebuilding democratic institutions.

For historians, diplomats, and politicians interested in the history of African dictators, Mugabe's reign serves as a cautionary tale. It highlights the dangers of unchecked power and the devastating consequences of repression on a nation and its people. Understanding Mugabe's repression and human rights abuses is crucial for preventing similar atrocities in the future and promoting democracy and human rights across the African continent.

The Ouster and Legacy of Robert Mugabe

Title: The Ouster and Legacy of Robert Mugabe

Introduction:

The chapter titled "The Ouster and Legacy of Robert Mugabe" delves into the life and reign of one of Africa's most notorious dictators. This subchapter provides a comprehensive account of Mugabe's rise to power, his controversial rule, and the events that led to his eventual ouster. By examining the political, social, and economic consequences of his leadership, this subchapter aims to shed light on Mugabe's lasting impact on Zimbabwe and its people.

Content:

Robert Mugabe, the first prime minister and later president of Zimbabwe, came to power in 1980 after decades of struggle against colonial rule. Initially hailed as a hero and champion of independence, Mugabe's leadership soon took a dark turn. Under his regime, Zimbabwe witnessed a steady erosion of democratic institutions, widespread human rights abuses, and a deteriorating economy.

Mugabe's rule was characterized by a series of controversial policies and actions. The forcible seizure of white-owned farms, known as the "land reform program," resulted in widespread economic disruption and food shortages. Mugabe's consolidation of power through intimidation, manipulation of elections, and suppression of dissent further undermined Zimbabwe's democratic foundations.

The ouster of Robert Mugabe in 2017 marked a turning point in Zimbabwe's history. Amid mounting discontent and a power struggle within his ruling party, Mugabe was forced to resign after nearly four decades in power. His removal was met with mixed reactions, with some celebrating the end of an oppressive regime, while others expressed concerns about the uncertain future of the country.

Mugabe's legacy is a complex and divisive subject. While he is revered by some as a symbol of African nationalism and resistance against colonialism, his autocratic rule and economic mismanagement have left a lasting impact. The country's once-thriving economy was decimated, with hyperinflation, unemployment, and poverty reaching alarming levels. Zimbabwe's healthcare and education systems also suffered greatly under Mugabe's rule.

Conclusion:

"The Ouster and Legacy of Robert Mugabe" provides an in-depth exploration of Mugabe's rise to power, his controversial rule, and his eventual downfall. By examining the political, social, and economic consequences of his leadership, this subchapter seeks to contribute to a comprehensive understanding of Zimbabwe's history. For historians, diplomats, and politicians interested in the rise and fall of notorious African dictators, this subchapter offers valuable insights into the turbulent reign of Robert Mugabe and its lasting impact on Zimbabwe and its people.

Chapter 5: History of the Rise and Fall of Muammar Gaddafi (Libya)

Gaddafi's Early Life and Revolutionary Ideals

Muammar Gaddafi, the former dictator of Libya, was born on June 7, 1942, in the small desert town of Sirte. His early life was marked by humble beginnings, growing up in a Bedouin family that lived a nomadic lifestyle. Despite his modest background, Gaddafi showed great ambition and determination from a young age.

Gaddafi's revolutionary ideals can be traced back to his early years as a student. After graduating from secondary school, he enrolled at the Benghazi Military Academy, where he developed a strong interest in politics and nationalism. It was during this time that he became acquainted with the works of influential thinkers such as Gamal Abdel Nasser, Karl Marx, and Frantz Fanon, who greatly influenced his revolutionary ideology.

In 1969, Gaddafi rose to power through a military coup that overthrew King Idris I. He established the Libyan Arab Republic and proclaimed himself as the "Brotherly Leader and Guide of the Revolution." Gaddafi's political ideology, known as "Third Universal Theory," aimed to create a socialist and pan-Arab state, promoting Arab unity and self-sufficiency.

Gaddafi implemented various policies to realize his revolutionary ideals. He nationalized Libya's oil industry, redistributing wealth and investing in social programs such as education and healthcare. He also sought to eliminate Western influence in Libya by expelling foreign military bases and promoting an indigenous form of Islamic socialism.

However, Gaddafi's revolutionary ideals soon turned into a ruthless dictatorship. He suppressed political dissent, silenced opposition, and established a pervasive surveillance system to maintain control over the population. Gaddafi's regime became notorious for its human rights abuses, including arbitrary arrests, torture, and extrajudicial killings.

Internationally, Gaddafi pursued an aggressive foreign policy, supporting various militant groups and sponsoring acts of terrorism. His involvement in the Lockerbie bombing in 1988, which resulted in the deaths of 270 people, further isolated him from the international community.

Gaddafi's revolutionary ideals ultimately led to his downfall. In 2011, a wave of popular protests swept across the Arab world, known as the Arab Spring. Libya was not spared from this uprising, as protesters demanded an end to Gaddafi's oppressive regime. The ensuing conflict culminated in a NATO-led intervention and Gaddafi's capture and killing in October 2011.

Gaddafi's early life and revolutionary ideals provide valuable insights into the rise and fall of one of Africa's most notorious dictators. His story serves as a cautionary tale, highlighting the dangers of unchecked power and the consequences of pursuing revolutionary ideals without regard for human rights and democratic principles.

Gaddafi's Rise to Power and Creation of the Libyan Jamahiriya

Muammar Gaddafi's rise to power and the subsequent creation of the Libyan Jamahiriya marked a significant chapter in the history of Africa's notorious dictators. This subchapter delves into the intricate details of Gaddafi's ascent to power, shedding light on the key events and ideologies that shaped his regime.

Gaddafi, born in a remote desert town in 1942, emerged as a charismatic and enigmatic figure on the African political landscape.

His rise to power can be traced back to September 1, 1969, when he and a group of military officers staged a bloodless coup, overthrowing King Idris I. This marked the end of the monarchy and the beginning of Gaddafi's authoritarian rule.

Under Gaddafi's leadership, Libya underwent a radical transformation. He envisioned a unique form of government called the Jamahiriya, which aimed to create a state where power was vested in the people, rather than traditional political institutions. Gaddafi saw himself as a revolutionary leader and the embodiment of the will of the Libyan people.

The creation of the Libyan Jamahiriya was marked by the implementation of Gaddafi's ideology, as outlined in his Green Book. This book outlined his vision for a stateless society, with power being decentralized and vested in the hands of the people through direct democracy. However, critics argued that this system merely served as a facade for Gaddafi's autocratic rule, as power remained concentrated in his hands.

Gaddafi's reign was characterized by a mixture of political repression, economic mismanagement, and support for international terrorism. He ruthlessly suppressed any dissent and maintained a tight grip on power through his Revolutionary Committees, secret police, and widespread surveillance. The regime's human rights abuses were well-documented, with reports of torture, disappearances, and extrajudicial killings.

Internationally, Gaddafi's regime was notorious for its support of terrorist organizations, such as the Irish Republican Army and the Palestine Liberation Organization. The 1988 bombing of Pan Am Flight 103 over Lockerbie, Scotland, which claimed the lives of 270 people, further tarnished Gaddafi's reputation and led to international sanctions against Libya.

Gaddafi's reign came to a tumultuous end in 2011 during the Arab Spring. His brutal crackdown on peaceful protests sparked a full-blown civil war, with NATO intervening on the side of the rebels. Gaddafi was captured and killed by rebel forces in October 2011, bringing an end to his 42-year autocratic rule.

In conclusion, Gaddafi's rise to power and the creation of the Libyan Jamahiriya were marked by a unique blend of ideology, repression, and international controversy. His regime left a lasting impact on Libya and the wider African continent, serving as a cautionary tale of the dangers of unchecked dictatorships. Understanding Gaddafi's rise and fall is crucial for historians, diplomats, and politicians seeking to navigate the complex history of Africa's notorious dictators.

Gaddafi's International Relations and Support for Terrorism

Muammar Gaddafi, the notorious dictator of Libya, was known for his controversial international relationships and support for terrorism. This subchapter aims to shed light on Gaddafi's international alliances, his involvement in acts of terrorism, and the impact it had on his regime and the global community.

Gaddafi's foreign policy was marked by a desire to challenge Western influence and establish himself as a prominent figure on the international stage. He sought alliances with other dictators, revolutionaries, and terrorist organizations that shared his anti-Western sentiments. Gaddafi provided financial and logistical support to various terrorist groups, such as the Irish Republican Army (IRA), the Palestine Liberation Organization (PLO), and the Revolutionary Armed Forces of Colombia (FARC).

One of Gaddafi's most infamous acts of terrorism was the bombing of Pan Am Flight 103 over Lockerbie, Scotland, in 1988. This tragic event claimed the lives of 270 people and led to years of investigation and diplomatic tensions between Libya and the West. Eventually, Gaddafi accepted responsibility for the attack and agreed to compensate the victims' families, leading to the lifting of international sanctions against Libya.

Gaddafi's support for terrorism also extended to African countries. He backed rebel groups in neighboring Chad and Sudan, fueling conflicts and instability in the region. His involvement in the Liberian civil war, supporting Charles Taylor's regime, further highlighted his disregard for human rights and his willingness to support brutal leaders.

Despite his controversial actions, Gaddafi managed to maintain certain international relationships. He forged alliances with other African dictators, such as Robert Mugabe of Zimbabwe and Mengistu Haile Mariam of Ethiopia, who shared his anti-Western sentiments. Gaddafi's Pan-Africanist ideology resonated with some African nations, and he used his oil wealth to provide financial assistance to various African countries, further solidifying his influence in the region.

Gaddafi's international relations and support for terrorism had significant consequences for his regime and the global community. While it bolstered his influence among like-minded dictators and revolutionaries, it also isolated him from the international community and led to years of sanctions and diplomatic tensions. Ultimately, Gaddafi's support for terrorism played a role in his downfall, as it fueled the rebellion that eventually overthrew his regime in 2011.

In conclusion, Gaddafi's international relations and support for terrorism were defining aspects of his regime. His alliances with other dictators and terrorist organizations, as well as his involvement in acts of terrorism, had far-reaching consequences both for his regime and the global community. Understanding these dynamics is crucial in comprehending the rise and fall of Muammar Gaddafi and the impact of his reign on African history.

Gaddafi's Suppression of Dissent and Human Rights Violations

Muammar Gaddafi, the former dictator of Libya, was widely known for his brutal suppression of dissent and flagrant human rights violations. This subchapter delves into the dark reign of Gaddafi, examining the methods he employed to maintain his grip on power and the impact it had on the Libyan people.

Gaddafi ruled Libya for over four decades, from 1969 until his overthrow and subsequent death in 2011. During his regime, he employed a combination of fear, violence, and propaganda to suppress any opposition and maintain absolute control. Dissent was ruthlessly crushed, and any form of criticism or opposition was met with severe consequences.

One of the most notorious incidents that highlighted Gaddafi's disregard for human rights was the 1996 Abu Salim prison massacre. Over 1,200 political prisoners were killed in a single day, with reports of torture and executions. This event served as a chilling reminder of the lengths Gaddafi was willing to go to silence his critics and maintain his iron grip on power.

Gaddafi also established a vast network of informants and secret police, ensuring that no dissenting voices would go unnoticed. This pervasive surveillance system created an atmosphere of constant fear and paranoia, with citizens hesitant to express their true opinions or engage in any form of political activism.

Freedom of expression was virtually non-existent under Gaddafi's rule. Independent media outlets were banned, and the state-controlled media acted as a propaganda tool to promote Gaddafi's ideology and glorify his regime. Journalists who dared to question or report on the government's actions faced harassment, imprisonment, or even disappearance.

The subchapter also explores the impact of Gaddafi's suppression of dissent on the Libyan people. It delves into the long-lasting psychological trauma endured by those who lived under his oppressive rule, as well as the stifling effect it had on intellectual and political discourse within the country.

Addressed to historians, diplomats, and politicians, this subchapter aims to shed light on the extent of Gaddafi's human rights violations and the consequences they had on Libya. By examining his reign within the broader context of African dictators, it provides valuable insights into the history of notorious despots and their impact on the continent. Ultimately, it serves as a reminder of the importance of safeguarding human rights and the need for accountability in the face of oppressive regimes.

The Fall of Gaddafi and the Aftermath in Libya

The fall of Muammar Gaddafi, the notorious dictator of Libya, marked a pivotal moment in the country's history and had far-reaching consequences not only for Libya but also for the entire African continent. This subchapter delves into the events leading up to Gaddafi's downfall and the aftermath that unfolded in Libya.

Gaddafi's rule was characterized by autocracy, repression, and a cult of personality that lasted for over four decades. His regime was notorious for its human rights abuses, suppression of political dissent, and the amassing of vast wealth at the expense of the Libyan people. However, in 2011, a wave of pro-democracy protests swept across the Arab world, commonly known as the Arab Spring, which ultimately reached Libya's shores.

Inspired by the uprisings in neighboring countries, Libyan citizens took to the streets demanding political reform and an end to Gaddafi's oppressive rule. What initially began as peaceful demonstrations quickly escalated into a full-scale civil war as Gaddafi brutally suppressed the uprising. The intervention of NATO forces further complicated the conflict, leading to a protracted and bloody struggle.

In October 2011, after months of intense fighting, Gaddafi was captured and killed by rebel forces, marking the end of his tyrannical reign. While many celebrated his demise as a triumph for democracy and human rights, the aftermath of Gaddafi's fall presented significant challenges for the country.

In the absence of a strong central authority, Libya descended into chaos, with various armed factions vying for control. The power vacuum allowed extremist groups, such as ISIS, to gain a foothold in the country, posing a threat not only to Libya but also to regional stability. Moreover, the country's economy, heavily dependent on oil exports, suffered a severe blow, exacerbating social and economic hardships for the Libyan people.

The international community, including historians, diplomats, and politicians, faced the daunting task of helping Libya rebuild and establish a stable government. Efforts were made to support the formation of a unity government and promote national reconciliation. However, the road to stability and democracy has been arduous, with progress marred by setbacks and ongoing conflicts.

The fall of Gaddafi and the subsequent turmoil in Libya serve as a cautionary tale about the challenges of transitioning from dictatorship to democracy. It highlights the importance of international support, diplomacy, and a comprehensive understanding of the historical context in order to navigate the complex aftermath of a notorious dictator's downfall.

In conclusion, the fall of Muammar Gaddafi in Libya represented a significant turning point in African history. The consequences of his downfall have not only affected Libya but also had wider regional implications. Understanding the complexities of this event is crucial for historians, diplomats, and politicians working on the history of notorious African dictators and seeking to prevent similar outcomes in the future.

Chapter 6: History of the Rise and Fall of Mengistu Haile Mariam (Ethiopia)

Mengistu's Background and Role in the Ethiopian Revolution

Mengistu Haile Mariam, born on May 21, 1937, in Walayta, Ethiopia, played a significant role in the Ethiopian Revolution and subsequent dictatorial regime. His background and actions during this period are essential to understanding the rise and fall of Mengistu Haile Mariam.

Mengistu was born to a peasant family and experienced poverty and hardship in his early years. However, he managed to receive an education and joined the Ethiopian army in 1966. His military career quickly progressed, and he became a prominent figure within the armed forces.

In 1974, Ethiopia was facing significant political and economic challenges, leading to widespread unrest and protests against Emperor Haile Selassie's regime. The discontent eventually culminated in a military coup, known as the Ethiopian Revolution. Mengistu, along with other military officers, played a crucial role in overthrowing the emperor.

Following the coup, Mengistu emerged as one of the main leaders of the ruling military junta, known as the Derg. He served as the head of the Provisional Military Administrative Council, and in 1977, he assumed the position of Chairman of the Derg.

Once in power, Mengistu implemented radical policies aimed at transforming Ethiopia into a Marxist-Leninist state. He nationalized industries, collectivized agriculture, and suppressed political opposition. Mengistu's regime became notorious for its human rights abuses, including mass executions, forced relocations, and torture.

One of the darkest chapters in Ethiopia's history occurred under Mengistu's rule. From 1983 to 1985, his government implemented a brutal campaign called the "Red Terror." Tens of thousands of suspected political opponents were arrested, tortured, and killed during this period.

Internationally, Mengistu aligned himself with the Soviet Union and received significant military and economic aid. This support allowed him to suppress various separatist movements within Ethiopia, such as the Eritrean Liberation Front and the Tigrayan People's Liberation Front.

However, Mengistu's regime faced mounting challenges, both domestically and internationally. The economy deteriorated, and the Ethiopian people grew increasingly dissatisfied with his leadership. Additionally, the Tigrayan People's Liberation Front gained strength and eventually overthrew Mengistu's government in 1991.

Following his ousting, Mengistu fled to Zimbabwe, where he lived in exile until 2017. He was subsequently extradited to Ethiopia and convicted of genocide, crimes against humanity, and other charges. Despite his absence, the legacy of Mengistu Haile Mariam and the impact of his rule still shape Ethiopia's political and social landscape today.

In conclusion, Mengistu Haile Mariam's background and role in the Ethiopian Revolution are crucial to understanding the rise and fall of this notorious African dictator. His ascent to power, implementation of oppressive policies, and eventual downfall highlight the impact of his regime on Ethiopia and its people.

Mengistu's Marxist-Leninist Regime and the "Red Terror"

During the late 1970s and early 1980s, Ethiopia was under the rule of Mengistu Haile Mariam, a military officer who established a

Marxist-Leninist regime known for its brutal tactics and human rights abuses. This subchapter delves into the dark period in Ethiopian history known as the "Red Terror," shedding light on Mengistu's oppressive rule and the impact it had on the country.

Mengistu came to power in 1974 following a coup that overthrew Emperor Haile Selassie. Inspired by Marxist ideology, he aimed to transform Ethiopia into a communist state. However, Mengistu's vision quickly degenerated into a reign of terror characterized by widespread violence, political purges, and mass executions.

The "Red Terror" was the regime's infamous campaign to eliminate any perceived threats to Mengistu's rule. Thousands of individuals, including intellectuals, students, and political dissidents, were targeted, arrested, and subjected to torture, imprisonment, and extrajudicial killings. The regime utilized numerous tactics to instill fear in the population, including arbitrary arrests, forced confessions, and public executions.

As the violence escalated, Ethiopia became a nation gripped by fear. Informants infiltrated communities, turning friends and family members against one another. People lived in constant apprehension, uncertain who could be trusted. The regime's secret police, known as the Derg, operated with impunity, carrying out their brutal actions under the guise of maintaining revolutionary order.

The "Red Terror" not only resulted in the loss of countless lives but also left a lasting impact on Ethiopian society. Families were torn apart, communities were destroyed, and the country's cultural and intellectual heritage suffered greatly. Many Ethiopians were forced into exile, leaving behind a scarred nation.

Despite the atrocities committed during his rule, Mengistu managed to cling to power until 1991 when he was overthrown by rebel forces.

He subsequently fled to Zimbabwe, where he sought refuge and lived in exile.

The story of Mengistu's Marxist-Leninist regime and the "Red Terror" serves as a cautionary tale, highlighting the dangers of unchecked power and ideological extremism. It also underscores the importance of documenting and remembering the history of notorious African dictators, ensuring that the voices of the victims are heard and the lessons learned are not forgotten.

This subchapter provides historians, diplomats, and politicians with a comprehensive account of Mengistu Haile Mariam's regime, shedding light on a dark chapter in Ethiopian history. It also offers valuable insights for those interested in studying the rise and fall of other notorious African dictators, such as Idi Amin, Mobutu Sese Seko, and Robert Mugabe, among others.

Mengistu's Policies and the Ethiopian Famine

In the annals of African history, few events have had such a devastating impact as the Ethiopian famine of the 1980s. This tragic chapter, marked by widespread starvation and loss of life, is inseparable from the policies implemented by Mengistu Haile Mariam, the notorious dictator who ruled Ethiopia from 1974 to 1991. Understanding the connection between Mengistu's policies and the Ethiopian famine is crucial to comprehending the scale of this catastrophe.

Mengistu came to power following a military coup in 1974, promising a brighter future for the Ethiopian people. However, his regime swiftly descended into a brutal dictatorship. By implementing a series of misguided policies, Mengistu exacerbated the country's existing economic challenges and set the stage for the devastating famine that would follow.

One of the most significant factors contributing to the famine was Mengistu's disastrous agricultural policy. Under his rule, the government embarked on a misguided collectivization program, forcibly relocating millions of peasants into state-controlled farms known as "people's cooperatives." This policy disrupted traditional farming practices and resulted in a sharp decline in agricultural productivity. The lack of incentives for farmers, coupled with inadequate investment in infrastructure and technology, led to widespread food shortages.

Furthermore, Mengistu's regime prioritized military spending over investment in agriculture and social welfare. The Ethiopian government's resources were funneled towards a costly war with neighboring Somalia, leaving little to address the growing food crisis. Despite the mounting evidence of impending famine, Mengistu's regime remained indifferent to the suffering of its own people.

To make matters worse, Mengistu's policies exacerbated the effects of the drought that struck Ethiopia in the early 1980s. Instead of adequately preparing for the drought and implementing measures to mitigate its impact, the government ignored warnings and failed to provide sufficient relief to affected regions. As a result, millions of Ethiopians were left vulnerable to starvation and disease.

The Ethiopian famine of the 1980s stands as a stark reminder of the devastating consequences of dictatorship and misguided policies. Mengistu Haile Mariam's regime, characterized by a lack of empathy, mismanagement, and prioritization of military ambitions, directly contributed to the suffering of millions of Ethiopians. It serves as a cautionary tale for historians, diplomats, and politicians, highlighting the importance of responsible governance and prioritizing the well-being of the people above all else.

As we delve into the history of notorious African dictators, it is essential to comprehend the complex interplay between political decisions and their consequences. The Ethiopian famine under Mengistu's rule serves as a stark reminder that the choices made by those in power can have far-reaching and devastating effects on the lives of ordinary people. By studying the rise and fall of Mengistu and other dictators, we gain valuable insights into the fragility of nations and the importance of upholding democratic values, human rights, and a genuine concern for the welfare of the population.

Mengistu's Relations with the Soviet Union and Cuba

Mengistu Haile Mariam, the dictator who ruled Ethiopia from 1974 to 1991, had strong relations with both the Soviet Union and Cuba during his time in power. These alliances played a significant role in shaping his regime and its policies.

Mengistu's ties with the Soviet Union were particularly important. From the beginning of his rule, he aligned himself with the Soviet bloc, adopting a socialist ideology and implementing policies inspired by the Soviet model. The Soviet Union provided economic and military support to Ethiopia, helping Mengistu consolidate his power and modernize the country. The Soviets supplied weapons, military advisors, and financial aid, which enabled Mengistu to suppress internal opposition and fight against various rebel groups.

The relationship with Cuba also proved crucial for Mengistu's regime. In the late 1970s, Ethiopia faced a severe threat from Somali forces backed by the United States. Mengistu sought help from the Cuban government, which responded by sending thousands of troops to Ethiopia. The Cuban soldiers played a decisive role in repelling the Somali invasion, protecting Mengistu's regime, and stabilizing the country.

The Soviet and Cuban support allowed Mengistu to pursue his policies of centralization and collectivization, aimed at transforming Ethiopia into a socialist state. These policies, however, had devastating consequences. Forced relocations, mass executions, and widespread human rights abuses characterized Mengistu's rule, which resulted in the deaths of an estimated 1.5 to 2 million Ethiopians.

Mengistu's reliance on the Soviet Union and Cuba also had implications for regional politics. Ethiopia became a key player in the Cold War dynamics of the Horn of Africa, with Mengistu supporting various rebel groups in neighboring countries, including Eritrea, Sudan, and Somalia. These interventions often worsened existing conflicts and contributed to instability in the region.

In summary, Mengistu Haile Mariam's relations with the Soviet Union and Cuba were essential in shaping his regime and its policies. The support he received from these allies enabled him to consolidate his power, suppress opposition, and pursue his socialist agenda. However, the consequences of these alliances were disastrous for Ethiopia, leading to widespread human rights abuses and regional instability. Understanding the dynamics of Mengistu's relationships with the Soviet Union and Cuba is crucial for historians, diplomats, and politicians interested in the history of notorious African dictators and the rise and fall of authoritarian regimes on the continent.

The Overthrow and Trial of Mengistu Haile Mariam

Mengistu Haile Mariam, one of the most notorious African dictators, ruled Ethiopia with an iron fist for nearly two decades. His reign, characterized by brutal repression and human rights abuses, came to an end in 1991, when he was overthrown by rebel forces.

Mengistu's rise to power began in 1974, during a period of political and social unrest in Ethiopia. As a high-ranking military officer, he played a key role in the coup that ousted Emperor Haile Selassie. Taking advantage of the power vacuum, Mengistu emerged as the leader of the Marxist-Leninist Derg regime.

Under Mengistu's rule, Ethiopia experienced widespread violence and economic decline. Dissent was crushed, and political opponents were subjected to torture, imprisonment, and execution. The Red Terror campaign, launched in the late 1970s, resulted in the deaths of tens of thousands of Ethiopians.

However, Mengistu's grip on power began to weaken in the 1980s. The economy was in shambles, with widespread famine and poverty gripping the country. The Ethiopian people grew increasingly disillusioned with their dictator, and rebel forces, led by the Ethiopian People's Revolutionary Democratic Front (EPRDF), gained momentum.

In 1991, the EPRDF launched a final offensive against Mengistu's regime, culminating in the capture of the capital, Addis Ababa. Mengistu fled to Zimbabwe, where he was granted asylum by President Robert Mugabe, another notorious African dictator.

Despite his exile, Mengistu's reign of terror would not go unpunished. In 2006, he was convicted in absentia by an Ethiopian court of genocide, crimes against humanity, and war crimes. The trial shed light on the extent of his atrocities, and the Ethiopian people finally had some semblance of justice.

Today, Mengistu Haile Mariam remains a controversial figure in Ethiopian history. While some view him as a hero for his role in overthrowing a corrupt monarchy, others see him as a ruthless dictator responsible for the deaths of hundreds of thousands of innocent people.

The overthrow and trial of Mengistu Haile Mariam serves as a stark reminder of the rise and fall of African dictators. It highlights the importance of holding leaders accountable for their actions and the inherent struggle for democracy and human rights in the continent.

For historians, diplomats, and politicians, studying the overthrow and trial of Mengistu offers valuable insights into the complexities of African politics and the challenges faced in transitioning from dictatorship to democracy. It also provides a comparative perspective on the rise and fall of other notorious African dictators, such as Idi Amin, Mobutu Sese Seko, and Muammar Gaddafi, among others.

Understanding the history of these dictators is crucial in preventing the repetition of past atrocities and fostering a more democratic and accountable future for Africa.

Chapter 7: History of the Rise and Fall of Charles Taylor (Liberia)

Taylor's Early Life and Involvement in Liberian Politics

In order to fully understand the rise and fall of notorious African dictator Charles Taylor, it is essential to delve into his early life and his involvement in Liberian politics. Born on January 28, 1948, in Arthington, Liberia, Taylor's childhood was marked by both privilege and tragedy.

Taylor hailed from a prominent Americo-Liberian family, descendants of freed African-American slaves who settled in Liberia in the early 19th century. His father was a renowned lawyer and his mother a member of the influential True Whig Party. However, tragedy struck when Taylor's father was accused of embezzlement and sentenced to prison, leading to financial struggles for the family.

In his youth, Taylor displayed charisma and a keen intellect, which eventually gained him a scholarship to study in the United States. There, he attended Bentley College in Massachusetts, where he developed a deep interest in politics and revolutionary movements. It was during this time that Taylor became exposed to the ideologies of various revolutionary leaders, including Che Guevara and Fidel Castro.

Upon his return to Liberia in 1980, Taylor found the country embroiled in political turmoil following the military coup led by Samuel Doe. Taking advantage of the chaos, Taylor formed an armed rebel group known as the National Patriotic Front of Liberia (NPFL) in 1989, with the aim of overthrowing Doe's regime.

Taylor's involvement in Liberian politics quickly escalated into a brutal civil war that ravaged the country for over a decade. The conflict claimed the lives of an estimated 250,000 people and displaced countless others. Taylor's forces were infamous for their ruthless tactics, including the recruitment of child soldiers and the perpetration of widespread human rights abuses.

Despite international condemnation, Taylor managed to gain support from neighboring countries and secure control over large parts of Liberia. In 1997, he was elected president in a highly contested and controversial election. However, his presidency was marred by corruption, economic mismanagement, and continued human rights violations.

Taylor's reign of terror eventually came to an end in 2003 when he was indicted by the Special Court for Sierra Leone for war crimes and crimes against humanity. He was subsequently arrested and brought to trial in The Hague, where he was found guilty in 2012 and sentenced to 50 years in prison.

The early life and involvement in Liberian politics of Charles Taylor offer valuable insights into the rise and fall of this notorious African dictator. His journey from a privileged background to becoming a key figure in one of Africa's bloodiest conflicts serves as a cautionary tale about the dangers of unchecked power and the devastating consequences of political instability.

Taylor's Role in the First Liberian Civil War

The first Liberian Civil War, which lasted from 1989 to 1997, was a devastating conflict that resulted in the loss of thousands of lives and left the country in ruins. At the center of this brutal conflict was Charles Taylor, a notorious African dictator whose rise to power and subsequent actions had a profound impact on the course of Liberian history.

Charles Taylor rose to prominence in the late 1980s as a rebel leader, leading the National Patriotic Front of Liberia (NPFL) in an armed rebellion against the then-president, Samuel Doe. Taylor's role in the conflict was marked by extreme violence and brutality, as he employed ruthless tactics to gain control over vast territories in Liberia.

Taylor's involvement in the war was characterized by his ability to manipulate and exploit ethnic tensions within the country. He capitalized on the longstanding grievances between the dominant Americo-Liberian elite and the indigenous tribes, using these divisions to rally support for his cause. Taylor's charisma and ability to present himself as a champion of the marginalized masses allowed him to amass a significant following, which ultimately helped him seize power.

During the war, Taylor was not only responsible for leading his forces in battles against the government, but he also engaged in widespread human rights abuses. Reports of massacres, rape, and mutilations carried out by his forces were rampant, leading to a humanitarian crisis of immense proportions. Taylor's reign of terror created a climate of fear and instability, leaving the country in a state of chaos.

Despite the atrocities committed by Taylor and his forces, he managed to consolidate his power and was eventually elected as the President of Liberia in 1997. However, his presidency was marked by corruption, economic mismanagement, and continued human rights violations. The international community, appalled by his actions, imposed sanctions on Liberia, further isolating the country and exacerbating its problems.

In 2003, under mounting pressure, Taylor was forced to step down and go into exile in Nigeria. He was later arrested and brought before the Special Court for Sierra Leone, where he was charged with war crimes and crimes against humanity. In 2012, Taylor was found guilty and sentenced to 50 years in prison.

Charles Taylor's role in the first Liberian Civil War serves as a stark reminder of the devastating consequences of unchecked power and the impact of dictators on the lives of ordinary people. His reign of terror left an indelible mark on Liberia, and the country continues to grapple with the aftermath of his rule. Understanding Taylor's role in this conflict is crucial for historians, diplomats, and politicians seeking to prevent similar atrocities in the future and promote peace and stability in Africa.

Taylor's Presidency and Support for Rebel Groups in Sierra Leone

During his presidency in Liberia from 1997 to 2003, Charles Taylor not only wrought havoc on his own country but also played a significant role in destabilizing neighboring Sierra Leone. This subchapter explores Taylor's presidency and his support for rebel groups in Sierra Leone, shedding light on the intricate web of violence and power struggles that characterized this period in West African history.

Taylor's rise to power in Liberia was marked by his involvement in the brutal civil war that ravaged the country from 1989 to 1997. As a warlord, he capitalized on the chaos and violence to amass power and wealth, eventually winning the 1997 presidential elections. However, his presidency was marred by corruption, human rights abuses, and the widespread looting of the country's natural resources, particularly diamonds.

In Sierra Leone, a bloody civil war was raging between the government forces and the Revolutionary United Front (RUF), a rebel group notorious for its brutal tactics, including amputations and the recruitment of child soldiers. Taylor saw an opportunity to expand his influence and bolster his own power by supporting the RUF financially, militarily, and logistically.

The support provided by Taylor's government to the RUF enabled the rebel group to sustain its campaign of terror and prolong the conflict in Sierra Leone. The illicit diamond trade played a crucial role in financing the RUF's activities, with Taylor allegedly providing a safe haven and facilitating the smuggling of conflict diamonds through Liberia. These diamonds were then exchanged for weapons and supplies, perpetuating the cycle of violence.

Taylor's support for rebel groups not only exacerbated the suffering of the Sierra Leonean people but also drew international condemnation and scrutiny. The United Nations and various human rights organizations accused Taylor of war crimes, including the recruitment of child soldiers and the use of rape as a weapon of war.

In 2003, under mounting pressure from regional and international actors, Taylor was forced to step down as president and went into exile in Nigeria. He was later arrested and brought before the Special Court for Sierra Leone, where he faced charges of war crimes, crimes against humanity, and violations of international humanitarian law.

The story of Taylor's presidency and his support for rebel groups in Sierra Leone serves as a cautionary tale, highlighting the destructive consequences of unchecked power and the devastating impact of regional conflicts. It underscores the importance of international cooperation and accountability in preventing the rise and fall of notorious African dictators like Taylor.

Taylor's Indictment and Trial at the International Criminal Court

The subchapter on Taylor's indictment and trial at the International Criminal Court sheds light on one of the most significant moments in the history of notorious African dictators. Charles Taylor, the former President of Liberia, became the first African head of state to be indicted and tried for war crimes and crimes against humanity by an international tribunal.

Taylor's rise to power was marked by brutality and violence. He led a rebel group, the National Patriotic Front of Liberia (NPFL), which ignited a civil war that ravaged the country for years. During his presidency from 1997 to 2003, Taylor's regime was characterized by corruption, human rights abuses, and the involvement in the illicit diamond trade, which fueled conflicts in neighboring Sierra Leone and Guinea.

The indictment of Taylor by the Special Court for Sierra Leone in 2003 was a groundbreaking moment. He was charged with 11 counts, including acts of terrorism, murder, rape, sexual slavery, and the recruitment and use of child soldiers. The international community saw this as an important step towards justice and accountability for the victims of the atrocities committed during the conflicts in West Africa.

Taylor's trial at the International Criminal Court (ICC) began in 2007, held in The Hague, Netherlands. The trial was a highly anticipated event, attracting attention from historians, diplomats, and politicians worldwide. The prosecution presented a wide range of evidence, including testimonies from victims and former associates of Taylor, as well as documents and video footage that implicated him in the crimes.

During the trial, Taylor vehemently denied the charges against him, claiming that he had always sought peace and stability in Liberia and the region. His defense team argued that he had no control over the actions of rebel factions and that he should not be held responsible for their crimes.

However, in 2012, the ICC delivered its verdict, finding Taylor guilty on all counts. He was sentenced to 50 years in prison, sending a strong message that impunity for African dictators would no longer be tolerated.

Taylor's indictment and trial at the ICC not only brought justice to the victims but also served as a precedent for holding other African leaders accountable for their actions. It highlighted the importance of international justice in addressing the crimes committed by notorious African dictators and provided hope for a more just and stable future for the continent.

This subchapter will be of great interest to historians, diplomats, and politicians, as it provides a comprehensive account of Taylor's indictment and trial, placing it within the broader context of the rise and fall of other notorious African dictators. It also explores the implications of this landmark trial for the history of African dictatorships and the pursuit of justice on the continent.

The Legacy of Charles Taylor in Liberia

Charles Taylor, the former president of Liberia, left a lasting legacy that continues to shape the country and its people. As one of Africa's notorious dictators, Taylor's rise to power and subsequent fall from grace is a captivating story that deserves examination. This subchapter delves into the history, influence, and impact of Charles Taylor on Liberia, offering a comprehensive understanding of his reign.

Taylor's rise to power can be traced back to the Liberian Civil War, which began in 1989. Exploiting the political and social unrest, Taylor formed a rebel group known as the National Patriotic Front of Liberia (NPFL). Through a combination of military force and manipulation, Taylor eventually seized control of the country in 1997.

During his presidency, Taylor's regime was characterized by corruption, human rights abuses, and economic mismanagement. The Liberian people suffered immensely under his rule, as widespread poverty, violence, and political repression became the norm. Taylor's involvement in the diamond trade, particularly in neighboring Sierra Leone, further fueled conflict and instability in the region.

In 2003, Taylor's reign came to an end when he was indicted by the Special Court for Sierra Leone for war crimes and crimes against humanity. Faced with mounting international pressure, Taylor resigned and went into exile in Nigeria. He was later extradited to The Hague, where he faced trial for his alleged crimes.

The legacy of Charles Taylor in Liberia is a complicated one. On one hand, his rule left a trail of destruction and suffering. The scars of the civil war and his brutal tactics still haunt the country today. On the other hand, Taylor's downfall demonstrated that even the most powerful dictators can be held accountable for their actions.

Since Taylor's departure, Liberia has made significant strides towards democracy and stability. However, the country still grapples with the long-lasting effects of his rule. Rebuilding the nation's institutions, healing the wounds of war, and addressing the socio-economic challenges remain ongoing challenges for Liberia's leaders.

In conclusion, Charles Taylor's legacy in Liberia is a cautionary tale of the consequences of unchecked power and the importance of accountability. His reign serves as a stark reminder of the devastating impact that a ruthless dictator can have on a nation and its people. By examining Taylor's rise and fall, historians, diplomats, and politicians can gain valuable insights into the history of notorious African dictators and the challenges they pose to governance, peace, and development.

Chapter 8: History of the Rise and Fall of Jean-Bédel Bokassa (Central African Republic)

Bokassa's Background and Rise to Power

Jean-Bédel Bokassa, often referred to as the "Butcher of Bangui," was a notorious African dictator whose rise to power in the Central African Republic was marked by brutality and corruption. To truly understand Bokassa, one must delve into his background and the circumstances that paved the way for his tyrannical reign.

Born on February 22, 1921, in Bobangui, French Equatorial Africa (now the Central African Republic), Bokassa's early life was marred by poverty and instability. With limited access to education, he turned to the military as a means of escape. Bokassa joined the French army and fought in both World War II and the French Indochina War, gaining valuable experience and developing a taste for power.

Following the Central African Republic's independence from France in 1960, Bokassa swiftly rose through the ranks of the army, eventually seizing control in a coup d'état on January 1, 1966. Bokassa's rule was characterized by a combination of military force, political cunning, and a ruthless disregard for human rights.

Once in power, Bokassa consolidated his authority by systematically eliminating his political rivals and establishing a personality cult around himself. He declared himself President for Life and later crowned himself Emperor Bokassa I in a grandiose ceremony that bankrupted the nation. Bokassa's extravagant lifestyle, which included lavish palace renovations and a fondness for luxury cars and jewelry, further exacerbated the country's economic woes.

However, it was the brutal repression of Bokassa's regime that truly defined his rule. Dissent was met with harsh punishment, and reports of torture, disappearances, and extrajudicial killings became common. Bokassa's infamous act of brutality came to light in 1979 when he ordered the massacre of schoolchildren who had protested against the expensive uniforms his regime had mandated.

Bokassa's reign of terror ultimately came to an end in 1979 when he was overthrown by a French-led military intervention. He was forced into exile and later faced trial for various crimes, including murder and cannibalism. Although he was initially sentenced to death, his sentence was later commuted to life imprisonment.

Jean-Bédel Bokassa's rise to power and subsequent reign of terror serve as a chilling reminder of the dark side of African history. His story, like those of other notorious African dictators, is a cautionary tale of the devastating consequences that can arise when power is concentrated in the hands of a ruthless and corrupt leader. Understanding the rise and fall of figures like Bokassa is essential for historians, diplomats, and politicians alike, as it sheds light on the complex dynamics of power and the importance of safeguarding democratic institutions to prevent the rise of future tyrants.

Bokassa's Reign as Emperor and the Coronation Ceremony

In the annals of African dictators, few are as notorious as Jean-Bédel Bokassa, the self-proclaimed Emperor of the Central African Republic. Bokassa's reign, characterized by brutality, excess, and megalomania, left an indelible mark on the history of the continent. His coronation ceremony stands as a symbol of his tyrannical rule and the depths of his delusions.

Bokassa's rise to power began in 1966 when he staged a military coup, overthrowing President David Dacko. With the country firmly under his control, Bokassa embarked on a path of consolidating his power and transforming the Central African Republic into his personal fiefdom. He declared himself President for Life and in 1976, took the audacious step of crowning himself Emperor in a lavish ceremony that rivaled the grandeur of past European monarchs.

The coronation ceremony, held on December 4, 1977, was a spectacle carefully orchestrated to showcase Bokassa's newfound status as Emperor. The event was attended by an array of foreign dignitaries, including diplomats, politicians, and even a few African heads of state. Bokassa spared no expense in the preparations, spending millions of dollars on extravagant decorations, costumes, and a golden throne.

As the ceremony unfolded, Bokassa, resplendent in a regal crimson robe, ascended the throne and was presented with a bejeweled crown. He then proceeded to crown himself, symbolizing his divine right to rule. The event was marked by pomp and circumstance, with military parades, cultural performances, and a lavish banquet fit for a king.

However, beneath the glitz and glamour, Bokassa's reign was a reign of terror. He ruled with an iron fist, suppressing any dissent and brutally suppressing opposition. Reports of torture, arbitrary arrests, and executions were widespread, as Bokassa sought to maintain absolute control over his subjects.

Bokassa's reign as Emperor came to an end in 1979 when he was overthrown by French-backed forces and exiled. The extent of his excesses and human rights abuses were revealed to the world, leading to widespread condemnation. The coronation ceremony, once seen as a symbol of Bokassa's power, became a testament to the depths of his tyranny.

The reign of Jean-Bédel Bokassa serves as a cautionary tale of the dangers of unchecked power and the lengths to which dictators will go to maintain their rule. His coronation ceremony, though opulent, was ultimately a facade that masked the suffering and oppression of his people. It stands as a stark reminder of the need for vigilant oversight and accountability in the face of autocratic regimes.

For historians, diplomats, and politicians, delving into the history of Bokassa's reign and the coronation ceremony provides valuable insights into the rise and fall of notorious African dictators. Understanding the motivations, methods, and consequences of their rule is crucial in preventing similar atrocities from occurring in the future.

Bokassa's Repressive Rule and Human Rights Violations

In the annals of African history, few dictators have left as indelible a mark as Jean-Bédel Bokassa, the self-proclaimed Emperor of the Central African Republic. Bokassa's reign, which lasted from 1966 to 1979, was characterized by a brutal and repressive regime, marked by egregious human rights violations.

Under Bokassa's rule, the Central African Republic witnessed a systematic erosion of civil liberties and a complete disregard for the rule of law. Dissent was stifled, political opposition was crushed, and the media was tightly controlled. Bokassa's regime employed a vast network of secret police and informants, ensuring that anyone suspected of opposing the government would swiftly face imprisonment, torture, or even death.

The most infamous episode of Bokassa's repressive rule occurred in 1979, when he declared himself Emperor and staged a lavish coronation ceremony modeled after Napoleon Bonaparte. The ostentatious event, which cost the impoverished nation a staggering amount of money, exemplified Bokassa's megalomania and detachment from the suffering of his people.

During his reign, Bokassa's human rights violations extended beyond political repression. Reports of widespread torture, extrajudicial killings, and forced labor camps surfaced, painting a grim picture of life under his regime. The international community, including human rights organizations and foreign governments, condemned his actions, but Bokassa remained defiant, dismissing such criticism as Western interference.

It was only in 1979 when Bokassa's oppressive rule came to an end. A French-led military intervention ousted him from power, and he was subsequently convicted of murder and cannibalism, among other crimes. Despite his overthrow, the scars of Bokassa's reign continue to haunt the Central African Republic, as the country struggles to rebuild itself and heal from the trauma inflicted by his brutal regime.

Bokassa's story serves as a cautionary tale, highlighting the dangers of unchecked power and the devastating consequences of dictatorial rule. By examining his reign alongside other notorious African dictators such as Idi Amin, Mobutu Sese Seko, and Robert Mugabe, historians, diplomats, and politicians gain valuable insights into the complex dynamics of power, repression, and human rights abuses in the continent's history.

The rise and fall of Bokassa and his counterparts provide important lessons for the present and future, reminding us of the vital importance of defending and upholding human rights, promoting democracy, and preventing the rise of dictators who trample upon the rights and dignity of their own people. Only through a thorough understanding of history can we hope to prevent such atrocities from happening again.

Bokassa's Downfall and Exile

In the annals of African dictators, few names evoke as much infamy as Jean-Bédel Bokassa, the self-proclaimed emperor of the Central

African Republic. Bokassa's reign, marked by brutality, corruption, and megalomania, eventually led to his downfall and exile from power.

Born into a humble family, Bokassa rose through the ranks of the military to become the president of the Central African Republic in 1966. However, it wasn't long before his thirst for power and grandeur became apparent. In 1977, he declared himself the emperor of the Central African Empire in a lavish coronation ceremony that rivaled the grandeur of ancient monarchs.

Bokassa's reign was characterized by a reign of terror, with widespread human rights abuses and a culture of fear. Dissent was not tolerated, and anyone perceived as a threat to his authority was met with swift and brutal repression. The notorious "Bokassa Trials" saw hundreds of political opponents executed or imprisoned, while the rest of the population lived in a state of constant surveillance.

However, the emperor's excesses and extravagance eventually caught up with him. In 1979, a student protest against the high cost of school uniforms escalated into a full-blown revolt. The French government, who had supported Bokassa until then, saw an opportunity to remove him from power and protect their economic interests in the region.

French forces intervened, and within days, Bokassa's regime was toppled. He was arrested and faced charges of cannibalism, embezzlement, and the murder of schoolchildren. Although acquitted of the most serious charges, he was sentenced to death, which was later commuted to life imprisonment.

In 1993, Bokassa was released from prison and went into exile in France. He lived the rest of his life in relative obscurity, occasionally making headlines for his outlandish statements and attempts to rehabilitate his tarnished image. Bokassa died in 1996, leaving behind a legacy of cruelty and corruption that still haunts the Central African Republic to this day.

Bokassa's downfall serves as a cautionary tale of the dangers of unchecked power and the consequences of a leader's descent into tyranny. It reminds us of the importance of vigilance, accountability, and the need for strong institutions to prevent the rise of future dictators. As historians, diplomats, and politicians, it is our duty to learn from the mistakes of the past and work towards a more just and democratic future for Africa and the world.

The Legacy and Controversy Surrounding Jean-Bédel Bokassa

Jean-Bédel Bokassa, the self-proclaimed Emperor of Central Africa, is undoubtedly one of the most notorious figures in African history. His rise to power and subsequent fall from grace have left a lasting impact on the Central African Republic and the continent as a whole. This subchapter delves into the complex legacy and enduring controversy surrounding Bokassa's rule.

Bokassa's ascent to power began in 1965 when he staged a military coup, toppling President David Dacko. He quickly consolidated his authority and declared himself President. However, his thirst for power knew no bounds, and in 1976, he crowned himself Emperor, emulating the grandeur of Napoleon Bonaparte. This audacious move drew international condemnation and sparked controversy both within and outside the Central African Republic.

During his reign, Bokassa ruled with an iron fist, suppressing political dissent and amassing a vast personal fortune at the expense of his impoverished citizens. His regime was marked by rampant corruption, human rights abuses, and the persecution of political opponents. Bokassa's brutality reached its peak in 1979 when he ordered the massacre of hundreds of schoolchildren who had protested against his regime. This horrific event, known as the "Bokassa Massacre," shocked the world and further tarnished his already tainted reputation.

The international community turned a blind eye to Bokassa's atrocities for years, as he strategically aligned himself with various world powers, including France and the Soviet Union. However, his excesses eventually caught up with him, and in 1979, French forces, under the pretext of rescuing children held captive by Bokassa, overthrew him and restored Dacko to power. Bokassa was subsequently convicted of numerous crimes, including murder and cannibalism, although the latter charge has been widely disputed.

Despite his ignominious downfall, Bokassa's legacy continues to haunt the Central African Republic. The country has struggled to recover from the devastation wrought by his regime, grappling with political instability, economic stagnation, and ongoing violence. Bokassa's reign of terror also highlighted the complicity of external powers in supporting dictators for their own strategic interests, a pattern that has repeated itself throughout Africa's history.

The controversial figure of Jean-Bédel Bokassa serves as a cautionary tale, reminding us of the dangers of unchecked power and the devastating consequences of dictatorial rule. As historians, diplomats, and politicians, it is crucial that we study and understand the rise and fall of notorious African dictators like Bokassa to prevent such dark chapters from being repeated in the future. By delving into the complexities of their legacies, we can gain valuable insights into the forces that shape nations and work towards a more just and equitable world.

Chapter 9: History of the Rise and Fall of Yahya Jammeh (Gambia)

Jammeh's Early Life and Military Coup

In the fascinating subchapter titled "Jammeh's Early Life and Military Coup," we delve into the intriguing background and rise to power of Yahya Jammeh, one of Africa's most notorious dictators. This chapter is a valuable contribution to the book "Tyrants of Africa: A Comprehensive History of Notorious Dictators," catering to historians, diplomats, and politicians interested in understanding the history of African dictators and their impact on their respective nations.

Yahya Jammeh was born on May 25, 1965, in Kanilai, a small village in The Gambia. Coming from humble beginnings, Jammeh's early life was marked by poverty and hardship. However, his determination and ambition propelled him towards a career in the military. He joined the Gambian National Army at a young age and quickly rose through the ranks, displaying leadership qualities and an insatiable thirst for power.

The turning point in Jammeh's life came on July 22, 1994, when he led a successful military coup against the country's then-president, Dawda Jawara. The coup d'état, known as Operation No Compromise, brought Jammeh to power at the tender age of 29, making him the youngest head of state in Africa at the time.

Jammeh's military coup marked the beginning of his authoritarian rule, which would last for over two decades. Initially, he promised a new era of democracy and progress for The Gambia, promising to root out corruption and improve the lives of its citizens. However, it soon became evident that Jammeh's intentions were far from noble.

Once in power, Jammeh established a repressive regime characterized by human rights abuses, media censorship, and political suppression. Dissent was swiftly silenced, and opposition parties were banned. Jammeh manipulated the judicial system to consolidate his power and eliminate any potential threats to his rule.

Throughout his tenure, Jammeh's rule was marred by allegations of corruption, nepotism, and economic mismanagement. His flamboyant lifestyle and extravagant spending were in stark contrast to the dire living conditions experienced by the majority of Gambians.

This subchapter sheds light on Jammeh's early life, his ascent to power through a military coup, and the subsequent authoritarian rule that defined his presidency. By examining Jammeh's rise and fall, we gain valuable insights into the history of African dictators and the profound impact they have had on their nations.

This subchapter will appeal to historians, diplomats, and politicians interested in understanding the broader context of Jammeh's rule within the history of African dictators. It also caters to the niche audience interested in the rise and fall of notorious African dictators such as Idi Amin, Mobutu Sese Seko, Robert Mugabe, Muammar Gaddafi, Mengistu Haile Mariam, Charles Taylor, Jean-Bédel Bokassa, Omar al-Bashir, and Hissène Habré.

Jammeh's Authoritarian Rule and Consolidation of Power

Yahya Jammeh's reign as the president of The Gambia from 1994 to 2017 was marked by his ruthless authoritarian rule and his unwavering efforts to consolidate power. This subchapter delves deep into the history of Jammeh's rise to power, the tactics he employed to maintain control, and the eventual downfall of his regime.

Jammeh came to power in a military coup in 1994, overthrowing the democratically elected government. Initially, he promised to bring stability and prosperity to The Gambia, but it soon became evident that his intentions were far from noble. Jammeh swiftly silenced any opposition, cracking down on political dissidents, journalists, and human rights activists. His regime was characterized by widespread human rights abuses, including torture, extrajudicial killings, and arbitrary arrests.

To consolidate his power further, Jammeh manipulated the political system. He established the Alliance for Patriotic Reorientation and Construction (APRC), his own political party, which dominated the political landscape. Jammeh used the APRC to control the legislature, judiciary, and media, effectively eliminating any checks and balances on his authority.

Jammeh also utilized propaganda and fear tactics to maintain a grip on the population. State-controlled media constantly praised his leadership and portrayed him as a savior figure. Dissent was met with brutal repression, instilling a sense of fear among the citizens.

However, Jammeh's reign began to crumble in the face of mounting international pressure and growing opposition within the country. The international community, including human rights organizations and foreign governments, condemned Jammeh's human rights abuses. Economic mismanagement and corruption further eroded public support for his regime.

In 2016, Jammeh suffered a surprising defeat in the presidential elections, losing to Adama Barrow, the candidate of a united opposition. Despite initially refusing to step down, mounting pressure from regional leaders and the threat of military intervention forced Jammeh into exile in Equatorial Guinea.

Yahya Jammeh's authoritarian rule and consolidation of power had a profound impact on the history of The Gambia. His regime left a legacy of fear, repression, and economic stagnation. This subchapter provides a comprehensive account of Jammeh's rise to power, the tactics he employed to maintain control, and the eventual downfall of his regime. It serves as a valuable resource for historians, diplomats, and politicians interested in understanding the rise and fall of notorious African dictators and the broader historical context in which they operated.

Jammeh's Human Rights Abuses and Suppression of Dissent

In the annals of African history, few dictators have left as indelible a mark as Yahya Jammeh, the former president of The Gambia. Jammeh's reign, characterized by rampant human rights abuses and the ruthless suppression of dissent, stands as a stark reminder of the depths to which power can corrupt.

Throughout his 22-year rule, Jammeh demonstrated a complete disregard for the basic rights and freedoms of the Gambian people. Dissent was not tolerated under his regime, with opposition leaders, journalists, and activists routinely subjected to harassment, intimidation, and arbitrary arrests. Jammeh's secret police, the National Intelligence Agency (NIA), operated with impunity, using torture and extrajudicial killings as tools to silence any form of opposition.

One particularly chilling aspect of Jammeh's repression was his use of detention centers, such as the infamous Mile 2 prison, as sites of torture and abuse. Political prisoners were subjected to horrific treatment, including beatings, electrocution, and sexual violence. Many never emerged from these dungeons alive, disappearing without a trace. The fear of these detention centers loomed large over the Gambian population, effectively silencing any potential dissent.

Furthermore, Jammeh's regime was notorious for its suppression of the media. Journalists were routinely targeted and harassed, with newspapers shuttered and critical voices silenced. The few remaining independent media outlets were forced to operate under a constant threat of violence, censorship, and closure. This deliberate assault on press freedom ensured that Jammeh's narrative remained unchallenged, perpetuating a climate of fear and misinformation.

Not only did Jammeh trample on the rights of his own people, but he also displayed a complete disregard for regional and international norms. His government was implicated in numerous cases of enforced disappearances, extrajudicial killings, and torture. The international community, including human rights organizations and foreign governments, condemned his actions, but Jammeh remained defiant, dismissing their concerns as interference in Gambian affairs.

Ultimately, Jammeh's reign came to an end in 2017, when he was forced into exile following his defeat in the presidential elections. His departure marked a glimmer of hope for the Gambian people, who could finally begin to rebuild their lives and their shattered institutions. However, the scars of Jammeh's abuses will endure for generations, a painful reminder of the dark chapter in Gambian history.

As historians, diplomats, and politicians, it is crucial that we study and understand the rise and fall of notorious African dictators like Jammeh. By shining a light on their human rights abuses and suppression of dissent, we can work towards preventing such atrocities in the future and fostering a culture of accountability and respect for human dignity. Only by learning from the past can we hope to build a brighter and more just future for Africa and its people.

Jammeh's Relations with the International Community

Yahya Jammeh, the former president of The Gambia, ruled the country with an iron fist for over two decades. During his time in power, Jammeh's relations with the international community were often strained, characterized by human rights abuses, political repression, and a disregard for democratic principles. This subchapter aims to shed light on Jammeh's interactions with the global stage, highlighting the impact of his actions on the country and the responses he garnered from historians, diplomats, and politicians.

Jammeh's tenure was marked by numerous incidents that drew international condemnation. His regime was accused of widespread human rights abuses, including arbitrary arrests, torture, and extrajudicial killings. Such actions not only violated basic human rights but also strained Gambia's relations with the international community. Human rights organizations, diplomats, and politicians consistently criticized Jammeh's oppressive tactics, calling for accountability and justice.

Furthermore, Jammeh's refusal to relinquish power after losing the 2016 presidential election further deteriorated his relations with foreign nations. The international community, including the African Union and the United Nations, condemned his actions and demanded a peaceful transfer of power. Jammeh's defiance led to regional intervention, with neighboring countries threatening military action to remove him from office. Eventually, he was forced into exile, seeking refuge in Equatorial Guinea.

In the aftermath of Jammeh's departure, the international community supported efforts to hold him accountable for his crimes. The Gambian government, with the assistance of international organizations such as the International Criminal Court, initiated investigations into human rights abuses committed during his rule. This pursuit of justice aimed to provide closure for the victims and contribute to the broader understanding of Jammeh's dictatorship.

The case of Yahya Jammeh serves as a reminder of the challenges faced by historians, diplomats, and politicians in dealing with notorious

African dictators. It highlights the importance of international cooperation and the pursuit of justice in holding leaders accountable for their actions. Jammeh's relations with the international community were marred by human rights abuses and political repression, leaving a lasting impact on The Gambia's history.

In conclusion, this subchapter examines Yahya Jammeh's relations with the international community, emphasizing the strained ties resulting from his oppressive rule in The Gambia. It underscores the significance of his actions and their consequences, reflecting the broader context of notorious African dictators and their rise and fall. Historians, diplomats, and politicians studying the history of African dictators will find valuable insights into the complexities of Jammeh's interactions with the global stage.

The Fall and Exile of Yahya Jammeh

Yahya Jammeh, the former president of The Gambia, rose to power through a military coup in 1994. For over two decades, he ruled the small West African nation with an iron fist, suppressing dissent and maintaining control through fear and coercion. However, Jammeh's reign came to a dramatic end in 2017 when he was forced into exile, marking a significant turning point in the history of The Gambia and the downfall of yet another notorious African dictator.

Jammeh's regime was characterized by rampant human rights abuses, including extrajudicial killings, enforced disappearances, and torture. Opposition voices were silenced, and anyone perceived as a threat to Jammeh's authority was swiftly dealt with. His rule was marked by corruption and economic mismanagement, with the majority of the population living in poverty while he and his inner circle amassed enormous wealth.

The turning point for Jammeh came in December 2016 when he lost the presidential election to Adama Barrow, a political newcomer. Initially, Jammeh accepted the election results but soon changed his mind, refusing to step down and challenging the legitimacy of the outcome. This led to a tense political standoff, with regional and international actors pressuring Jammeh to respect the will of the Gambian people.

In a last-ditch attempt to cling to power, Jammeh declared a state of emergency and sought to challenge the election results in court. However, faced with mounting pressure from neighboring countries and the threat of military intervention, he eventually conceded defeat and agreed to step down in January 2017.

Jammeh's exile marked the end of an era for The Gambia. He fled to Equatorial Guinea, where he continues to live in luxurious exile, shielded from accountability for his crimes. The Gambian people, however, have embarked on a path of transitional justice, seeking to hold Jammeh and his accomplices accountable for their actions.

The fall and exile of Yahya Jammeh serves as a powerful reminder of the importance of democratic governance and the need to hold dictators accountable for their crimes. It is a cautionary tale for other African leaders who may be tempted to cling to power at the expense of their people's rights and aspirations.

In conclusion, the fall and exile of Yahya Jammeh represent a significant chapter in the history of notorious African dictators. It highlights the resilience of the Gambian people and their commitment to democratic values. Historians, diplomats, and politicians can learn from Jammeh's reign and its ultimate downfall, as well as the ongoing efforts of the Gambian people to achieve justice and reconciliation. This subchapter sheds light on the complex dynamics of power, corruption, and resistance in Africa's history, providing valuable insights into the rise and fall of dictators across the continent.

Chapter 10: History of the Rise and Fall of Omar al-Bashir (Sudan)

Al-Bashir's Background and Rise to Power

Omar al-Bashir, the former President of Sudan, was one of the most notorious African dictators in recent history. His rise to power and subsequent reign were marked by oppression, human rights abuses, and a devastating civil war that ravaged the country for decades.

Born on January 1, 1944, in Hosh Bannaga, Sudan, al-Bashir hailed from humble beginnings. He joined the Sudanese Army in 1960 and quickly rose through the ranks due to his military prowess and loyalty to the government. In 1989, he seized power through a military coup, overthrowing the democratically elected government of Prime Minister Sadiq al-Mahdi.

Al-Bashir's rise to power came at a time when Sudan was facing several challenges. The country was grappling with ethnic tensions, economic instability, and a long-standing civil war between the North and the South. Al-Bashir capitalized on these issues to consolidate his power and establish an authoritarian regime.

During his tenure, al-Bashir implemented Sharia law, which further marginalized non-Arab and non-Muslim communities in Sudan. This move escalated tensions and fueled the ongoing civil war. In the region of Darfur, al-Bashir's government waged a brutal campaign against rebel groups, resulting in widespread human rights abuses, including ethnic cleansing and genocide. The conflict in Darfur alone claimed the lives of hundreds of thousands of people and displaced millions.

Internationally, al-Bashir became a pariah. The International Criminal Court (ICC) issued two arrest warrants against him for war crimes,

crimes against humanity, and genocide committed in Darfur. Despite the charges, al-Bashir managed to evade arrest, largely due to the support he received from regional allies and Sudanese elites who benefited from his regime.

However, al-Bashir's grip on power began to weaken in 2019 when protests erupted across Sudan, demanding his resignation and an end to his oppressive rule. The Sudanese people, tired of decades of corruption and repression, took to the streets in massive numbers, forcing the military to intervene. In April 2019, al-Bashir was finally ousted from power, marking the end of his 30-year reign.

Al-Bashir's background and rise to power exemplify the characteristics of many African dictators. He exploited existing divisions within society, suppressed opposition, and manipulated the political and economic systems to consolidate his rule. His legacy is one of violence, suffering, and a fractured nation struggling to rebuild itself in the aftermath of his rule.

Al-Bashir's Rule and the Darfur Conflict

In the annals of African history, the reign of Omar al-Bashir stands as a stark reminder of the atrocities committed by dictators on the continent. Al-Bashir's rule over Sudan, which lasted from 1989 to 2019, was marred by violence, repression, and the infamous Darfur conflict.

During his time in power, al-Bashir employed a combination of military force, political manipulation, and religious rhetoric to consolidate his control over Sudan. He established an authoritarian regime that stifled dissent and curtailed civil liberties. Opposition parties were banned, journalists were censored, and political dissidents were systematically silenced through intimidation, arrest, and torture.

However, it was the Darfur conflict that brought international attention and condemnation upon al-Bashir's regime. The conflict erupted in 2003 when rebel groups from Darfur, a region in western Sudan, took up arms against the central government, accusing it of neglect and marginalization.

Al-Bashir's response to the rebellion was swift and brutal. He deployed government-backed militias known as the Janjaweed, who unleashed a campaign of terror upon the civilian population of Darfur. Villages were burned, women were raped, and thousands were killed. The United Nations estimates that more than 300,000 people lost their lives in the conflict, with millions more displaced.

The international community, horrified by the scale of violence, labeled the situation in Darfur as genocide. The International Criminal Court (ICC) issued arrest warrants for al-Bashir on charges of war crimes, crimes against humanity, and genocide. However, he remained defiant, refusing to surrender himself to the court.

Despite mounting pressure from the international community, it was not until 2019 that al-Bashir's rule finally came to an end. A popular uprising, fueled by economic hardship and political repression, forced him from power. The Sudanese people, tired of years of dictatorship and bloodshed, demanded a transition to democracy.

The legacy of al-Bashir's rule and the Darfur conflict continues to haunt Sudan. Rebuilding the country, healing the wounds, and establishing a just and inclusive society will be an arduous task. However, it is through understanding the history of notorious African dictators like al-Bashir that we can work towards preventing such atrocities in the future. As historians, diplomats, and politicians, it is our responsibility to learn from the past and strive for a better future for Africa and its people.

Al-Bashir's International Isolation and Indictment by the ICC

Omar al-Bashir, the former president of Sudan, stands as one of the most notorious African dictators in history. His reign, marked by brutal repression and gross human rights violations, resulted in his international isolation and eventual indictment by the International Criminal Court (ICC). This subchapter delves into the events that led to Al-Bashir's isolation and sheds light on the significance of his indictment by the ICC.

Al-Bashir's rise to power in Sudan was characterized by a military coup in 1989, overthrowing a democratically elected government. From the onset, his rule was marred by a disregard for human rights and a brutal crackdown on political dissidents. Opposition parties were banned, and any form of dissent was met with severe repression.

Internationally, Al-Bashir's regime faced increasing scrutiny due to its involvement in the conflict in Darfur. The Sudanese government, under his leadership, was accused of committing war crimes, crimes against humanity, and genocide against the people of Darfur. The international community, including historians, diplomats, and politicians, condemned these atrocities and called for accountability.

In 2009, the ICC issued an arrest warrant for Al-Bashir, charging him with crimes against humanity and war crimes. This marked a significant turning point in his international standing. Al-Bashir became the first sitting head of state to be indicted by the ICC, further isolating him from the global community.

Al-Bashir's indictment had far-reaching consequences. It limited his ability to travel internationally, as many countries were obligated to arrest and extradite him to the ICC if he set foot on their soil. This restricted his diplomatic engagements and undermined his credibility on the world stage.

Furthermore, the indictment fueled domestic opposition against Al-Bashir. Pro-democracy movements and civil society organizations seized the opportunity to demand his removal from power, using the ICC charges as evidence of his illegitimacy. The Sudanese people, inspired by the Arab Spring and driven by a desire for change, protested against his regime relentlessly.

Ultimately, Al-Bashir's international isolation and indictment played a pivotal role in his downfall. In 2019, after months of mass protests, he was ousted from power by the military, ending his three-decade-long rule. The ICC's indictment contributed to the erosion of his support base and weakened his grip on power.

The case of Omar al-Bashir stands as a reminder of the power of international justice and the importance of holding dictators accountable for their actions. It serves as a cautionary tale for other notorious African dictators, highlighting the consequences they may face when their crimes against humanity are exposed and international pressure mounts.

Al-Bashir's Ouster and the Transition in Sudan

The fall of Omar al-Bashir, the notorious dictator of Sudan, marked a significant turning point in the country's history. This subchapter delves into the events surrounding al-Bashir's ouster and the subsequent transitional period in Sudan. It provides a comprehensive analysis of the factors that led to his downfall and the challenges faced during the transition.

Omar al-Bashir's reign was characterized by a brutal and oppressive regime that lasted for three decades. His rule was marred by gross human rights violations, economic mismanagement, and corruption. However, in 2019, the people of Sudan took to the streets in mass protests, demanding an end to al-Bashir's regime. These protests, led by a diverse coalition of Sudanese citizens, including youth, women, and professionals, marked the beginning of a new era for the country.

The subchapter explores the key factors that contributed to the success of the protests, such as the role of social media in mobilizing and organizing the masses, as well as the resilience and determination of the Sudanese people. It also examines the international community's response to the crisis, particularly the pressure exerted by diplomats and politicians to support the protesters' demands for change.

Following al-Bashir's ouster, Sudan entered a transitional period, which posed its own set of challenges. The subchapter delves into the complex dynamics within the transitional government, the power struggles between different factions, and the delicate balancing act between civilian and military leadership. It also analyzes the steps taken by the transitional government to address the legacy of al-Bashir's regime, including the establishment of a commission to investigate human rights abuses and the initiation of economic reforms.

Furthermore, this subchapter highlights the role of regional and international actors in supporting Sudan during its transition. It examines the diplomatic efforts to secure financial aid and debt relief, as well as the challenges faced in rebuilding the country's shattered economy and addressing the grievances of marginalized regions.

Addressed to historians, diplomats, and politicians, this subchapter offers a comprehensive account of al-Bashir's ouster and the subsequent transition in Sudan. It provides valuable insights into the history of notorious African dictators, shedding light on the complexities of their rise and fall. By studying the case of Sudan, readers can gain a deeper understanding of the challenges and opportunities associated with political transitions in authoritarian regimes.

The Legacy and Challenges of Omar al-Bashir's Rule

Omar al-Bashir, the former President of Sudan, left a lasting legacy on the nation that continues to shape its present and future. Throughout his rule, which lasted for three decades from 1989 to 2019, al-Bashir's regime was characterized by autocracy, human rights abuses, and economic mismanagement. This subchapter delves into the complexities of his reign, exploring both the impact he had on Sudan and the challenges the country faces in the aftermath of his rule.

Under al-Bashir's leadership, Sudan experienced a multitude of challenges. His regime was marked by widespread corruption, economic mismanagement, and a disregard for human rights. The Sudanese people suffered from a lack of political freedoms, arbitrary arrests, torture, and repression. Furthermore, al-Bashir's government was responsible for the genocide in Darfur, which resulted in the deaths of hundreds of thousands of people and the displacement of millions.

One of the most significant legacies of al-Bashir's rule is the division of Sudan. During his tenure, the country faced multiple secessionist movements, most notably in South Sudan, which eventually gained independence in 2011. The secession of South Sudan not only fractured the nation but also intensified existing conflicts and further destabilized the region.

Another challenge that Sudan faces in the post-al-Bashir era is the economic crisis. Under his rule, the country experienced high levels of debt, inflation, and a lack of investment in key sectors. The mismanagement of resources and rampant corruption led to a deteriorating economy, leaving a legacy of poverty and unemployment for the Sudanese people.

In addition to these challenges, Sudan is also confronted with the task of transitioning to a democratic system. Al-Bashir's authoritarian rule suppressed political opposition and stifled the growth of democratic institutions. The current government, formed after his ousting, must navigate the delicate process of establishing a democratic framework and ensuring a peaceful transition of power.

For historians, diplomats, and politicians interested in the history of notorious African dictators, al-Bashir's rule provides a valuable case study. It offers insights into the complexities of autocratic regimes, the consequences of human rights abuses, and the challenges of post-conflict reconstruction and development.

In conclusion, the legacy and challenges of Omar al-Bashir's rule in Sudan are extensive and multifaceted. From political oppression and human rights abuses to economic mismanagement and regional destabilization, his reign has left a lasting impact on the nation. As Sudan moves forward, it must confront these challenges, striving to establish a democratic system, address economic crises, and heal the wounds of a divided nation.

Chapter 11: History of the Rise and Fall of Hissène Habré (Chad)

Habré's Early Life and Political Career

Hissène Habré, one of the notorious African dictators, was born on August 13, 1942, in Faya-Largeau, Chad. His early life saw him develop a strong sense of nationalism and anti-colonialism, which would later shape his political career. Growing up in a politically tumultuous environment, Habré witnessed the oppressive rule of French colonialists and the subsequent power struggles within Chad.

Habré's political journey began in the late 1960s when he joined the National Liberation Front (FROLINAT), a rebel group fighting against the Chadian government. FROLINAT aimed to end the autocratic rule of President François Tombalbaye and establish a more equitable society. Habré quickly rose through the ranks, displaying exceptional military and strategic skills.

In 1973, Habré shifted his allegiance and founded the Armed Forces of the North (FAN), a breakaway faction from FROLINAT. FAN's primary objective was to challenge the existing power structures and address the marginalization of northern Chadians. Habré's charisma and leadership abilities attracted a significant following, and FAN became a formidable force against the government.

Habré's political career reached its peak in 1982 when he overthrew President Goukouni Oueddei in a violent coup. He assumed control of Chad and became the country's president, consolidating his power through a repressive regime. Habré's rule was marked by widespread human rights abuses, including torture, arbitrary detentions, and extrajudicial killings. His government's security apparatus, known as the Documentation and Security Directorate (DDS), instilled fear and controlled the population through a network of informants.

Internationally, Habré positioned himself as a key player in regional politics. He aligned with the United States and France, portraying himself as a bulwark against Libyan influence in the region. However, his relations with neighboring countries, particularly Sudan and Libya, remained strained, leading to several conflicts and proxy wars.

Habré's political career eventually came to an end in 1990 when he was overthrown by current President Idriss Déby. Fleeing to Senegal, he lived in exile for over two decades before facing trial for crimes against humanity, war crimes, and torture. In 2016, Habré became the first African dictator to be convicted by an African Union-backed court, receiving a life sentence for his atrocities.

Hissène Habré's early life and subsequent political career highlight the complex dynamics of power, nationalism, and autocracy in Africa. His rise to power, marked by rebellion and violence, exemplifies the tumultuous nature of African politics during the era of notorious dictators. Understanding Habré's story is crucial for historians, diplomats, and politicians seeking to comprehend the broader history of African dictators and their impact on the continent's socio-political landscape.

Habré's Presidency and the Repressive DDS

Hissène Habré's presidency in Chad, from 1982 to 1990, was marred by a reign of terror enforced by the notorious Directorate of Documentation and Security (DDS). This subchapter delves into the dark period of Habré's rule and the atrocities committed by the DDS, shedding light on the rise and fall of yet another African dictator.

Habré seized power in a military coup and established a regime known for its brutal tactics to maintain control. The DDS, a secret police force he created, became the primary tool for suppressing dissent and enforcing his rule. Under the leadership of Habré's trusted ally, Saleh Younous, the DDS carried out widespread human rights abuses, including arbitrary arrests, torture, and extrajudicial killings.

The DDS operated a vast network of prisons, known as the "Chamber of Horrors," where political opponents, activists, and anyone perceived as a threat to Habré's regime were detained and subjected to unimaginable cruelty. Many prisoners were held incommunicado, without any legal representation or contact with the outside world. Countless individuals lost their lives or suffered lifelong physical and psychological traumas within the walls of these secret detention centers.

International human rights organizations, such as Amnesty International and Human Rights Watch, documented the atrocities committed by the DDS during Habré's presidency. However, it wasn't until years later that justice began to catch up with Habré and his henchmen. In 2013, Habré was arrested in Senegal and charged with crimes against humanity, war crimes, and torture. His trial in 2015 marked a significant milestone in the fight against impunity for African dictators.

This subchapter explores the historical context surrounding Habré's rise to power, his consolidation of control through the DDS, and the subsequent efforts to hold him accountable for the crimes committed under his regime. It provides a comprehensive analysis of the strategies employed by Habré to maintain power, his relationship with external actors, and the long-lasting impact of his presidency on Chad and its people.

For historians, diplomats, and politicians interested in the history of notorious African dictators, this subchapter offers valuable insights into the complex dynamics of power, repression, and accountability.

It serves as a reminder of the importance of documenting and understanding the rise and fall of such leaders to prevent history from repeating itself and to ensure justice for their victims.

Habré's Human Rights Violations and the Chadian-Tibesti Conflict

Hissène Habré, the former President of Chad, is widely known for his brutal human rights violations and his involvement in the Chadian-Tibesti Conflict. This subchapter delves into the atrocities committed under his regime and the impact of the conflict on Chad and its people.

Habré came to power in 1982 through a coup d'état and ruled with an iron fist until he was overthrown in 1990. During his reign, he established a reign of terror characterized by widespread torture, extrajudicial killings, and political repression. Thousands of Chadians were subjected to inhumane treatment, including arbitrary arrests, disappearances, and torture in the notorious prisons of Chad.

One of the most significant episodes during Habré's rule was the Chadian-Tibesti Conflict. The Tibesti region, located in the north of Chad, became a hotbed of conflict as various ethnic and rebel groups sought to challenge Habré's authority. Habré responded with brutal force, launching military campaigns that resulted in the displacement and death of countless civilians.

The conflict was marked by numerous human rights violations, including mass killings, sexual violence, and the destruction of entire villages. The people of Tibesti suffered greatly, enduring not only the direct consequences of the conflict but also the long-term effects of displacement, loss of livelihoods, and social disruption.

Habré's human rights abuses and the Chadian-Tibesti Conflict attracted international attention and condemnation. Human rights organizations and activists documented the atrocities committed under his regime, leading to calls for justice and accountability. Eventually, Habré's reign of terror came to an end when he was ousted from power and forced into exile.

In 2016, Habré was convicted of crimes against humanity, war crimes, and torture by a special court established in Senegal. This landmark trial marked a significant step towards justice for the victims of his regime and served as a powerful reminder of the importance of holding dictators accountable for their actions.

The Chadian-Tibesti Conflict remains a painful chapter in Chad's history, leaving scars that are yet to fully heal. However, it also serves as a testament to the resilience and determination of the Chadian people, who have shown remarkable strength in the face of adversity.

This subchapter will provide historians, diplomats, and politicians with a comprehensive understanding of Habré's human rights violations and the Chadian-Tibesti Conflict. It aims to shed light on the dark legacy of a notorious African dictator and the enduring impact of conflict on a nation's history.

11.

11. The Rise and Fall of Hissène Habré: A Tale of Tyranny and Justice

In the annals of African history, few dictators have left as indelible a mark as Hissène Habré. His reign of terror in Chad remains a chilling reminder of the depths to which power-hungry leaders can sink. This subchapter delves into the captivating story of Habré's rise to power, his iron-fisted rule, and, ultimately, his downfall.

Born in 1942 in Faya-Largeau, Chad, Habré emerged as a prominent figure during the turbulent era of post-independence. In 1982, he seized power through a coup, establishing himself as the President of Chad. Habré's regime was marked by ruthless tactics, including widespread human rights abuses, political repression, and the creation of a vast network of secret police.

Under Habré's rule, dissent was met with brutality. Thousands of Chadians were subjected to arbitrary arrests, torture, and extrajudicial killings. The notorious Directorate of Documentation and Security (DDS) became synonymous with fear and oppression, instilling a climate of terror across the nation.

However, Habré's iron grip on power was not destined to last. In 1990, a rebel coalition known as the Patriotic Salvation Movement launched a successful offensive, overthrowing Habré and forcing him into exile in Senegal. The end of his reign brought a glimmer of hope to the people of Chad, who had long suffered under his despotic rule.

But the story does not end there. Habré's victims refused to let him escape justice. After years of tireless efforts, human rights activists, historians, and legal experts rallied to hold him accountable for his crimes. In 2016, Habré was finally brought to trial before the Extraordinary African Chambers in Senegal.

The trial was a landmark moment, marking the first time an African dictator was prosecuted by another African country for grave human rights violations. Habré was found guilty of crimes against humanity, war crimes, and torture, and was sentenced to life in prison. The trial served as a powerful symbol of justice, demonstrating that even the most powerful tyrants can be held accountable for their actions.

The rise and fall of Hissène Habré stands as a cautionary tale, reminding us of the importance of preserving democracy and human rights. His story serves as a testament to the resilience of those who have suffered under tyranny and the unwavering commitment of historians, diplomats, and politicians to uncover the truth and seek justice.

www.ingramcontent.com/pod-product-compliance
Lightning Source LLC
Chambersburg PA
CBHW022035150726
47990CB00002B/973